Welcome to the 2025 BBC Proms

On behalf of the entire BBC Proms team, it is a privilege to introduce our 2025 season and to invite you to enjoy eight weeks of wonderful music-making, both at the Royal Albert Hall and in venues across the UK. As ever, some of the world's finest orchestras will be joining us, from the Vienna Philharmonic to the Leipzig Gewandhaus Orchestra. The backbone of the Proms, however, is the BBC's own ensembles, without which this festival simply would not exist. They play such a special role in the musical life of this country and I am hugely proud to be welcoming them to the Proms for a total of nearly 60 performances this year.

Even a festival spanning 130 years still has room for many 'firsts'. In 2025 these include debuts from artists ranging from the acclaimed young pianist Bruce Liu and the inspirational Nicholas McCarthy (who performs Ravel's Piano Concerto for the Left Hand in this, the composer's 150th-anniversary year) to the multi-Grammy Award-winning vocalist Samara Joy. As always, there will be many world-premiere performances: on the First Night we hear a new work by Master of the King's Music Errollyn Wallen, and on the Last Night it is the turn of Oscar-winning composer Rachel Portman.

This year's anniversaries include the centenaries of modernist icons Luciano Berio and Pierre Boulez. I am thrilled that the Ensemble intercontemporain, the ... ing to the Proms to celebrate his legacy. We also reflect on 50 years since the death of Shostakovich; celebrate Arvo Pärt's 90th birthday; and mark major anniversaries of both film composer Bernard Herrmann and the so-called 'Waltz King', Johann Strauss II.

Proms concerts outside London this year include our first visit to Sunderland, as part of our partnership with Gateshead's Glasshouse International Centre for Music. We also return to the Bristol Beacon, join forces with the Ulster Orchestra for a Prom in Belfast and celebrate Bradford's status as the UK City of Culture 2025.

There is so much more I could mention: *The Marriage of Figaro* from Glyndebourne, the CBeebies Prom, our two concerts with Sir Simon Rattle, the National Youth Orchestra performing *The Planets* – the list goes on. Last season brought BBC Radio 3 its largest audience in over three years, with the station attracting more listener hours per week than ever before. This year every Prom is once again broadcast on Radio 3 and available on BBC Sounds until 30 days after the Last Night.

I still remember the thrill of attending the BBC Proms for the first time as a 19-year-old student. Whether this is your first season, or you've been with us for years, I wish you a wonderful summer of live music. There really is nothing else like it.

Sam Jackson
Controller, BBC Radio 3 and BBC Proms

At a Glance

For Concert Listings, see pages 109–146 • For Contents, including details of feature articles, see overleaf

Period Drama

Two dynamic French early music groups present jewels of the Baroque and Renaissance. Le Consort and young violinist/director Théotime Langlois de Swarte make their Proms debuts, exploring Bach, Vivaldi and the composers' English counterparts. Returning for the first time since 2012 are Le Concert Spirituel and Hervé Niquet, whose programme features Striggio's 40-part motet (which inspired Tallis's famous *Spem in alium*), as well as his Mass in 40 and 60 parts: an extravagance from Renaissance Florence.

20 JULY, 17 AUGUST

Out and About

Expanding on its series of performances across the UK, the Proms deepens its links with Gateshead and Bristol with further weekend residencies, celebrating local musicians, fostering new collaborations and (in Gateshead) including the CBeebies Prom, Wildlife Jamboree, for families. Plus, there's a special edition of Radio 3's *'Round Midnight* in Sunderland, an evocative words-and-music event themed around Radio 4's *Shipping Forecast* in Belfast; and the first ever Prom in Bradford, with 'queen of African music' Angélique Kidjo and the BBC Philharmonic Orchestra marking the city's status as UK City of Culture 2025.

See pages 142–146

Faithful, or Traitor?

Deception, betrayal … murder. Claudia Winkleman presents a Proms celebration of the hit BBC reality show *The Traitors*, with a light-hearted look at music that reflects the dark underbelly of human nature. The event features big-screen footage and guest appearances from contestants, as well as the scandalously skilful BBC Scottish Symphony Orchestra and the sinfully silken-voiced BBC Singers.

26 JULY, 3pm & 7.30pm

Have Sitar, Will Travel

The ever-curious, free-ranging sitarist and composer Anoushka Shankar returns for her fifth Proms appearance, bringing the wide range of moods, places and artistic influences captured in her album trilogy *Chapters* – reimagined in new arrangements and cast into the orchestral arena.

12 AUGUST *(See also pages 64–66)*

Dear Dmitry

We may never untangle Dmitry Shostakovich's complex relationship with the Soviet regime, but with music that wavers between wild energy, haunting desolation and wry humour, it's fine to be kept guessing. Works featured in this focus, 50 years after the composer's death, include the opera *The Lady of Macbeth of the Mtsensk District* (banned by Stalin) and the Fifth Symphony (a plea for forgiveness), as well as the buzzing *Festive Overture* and witty *Suite for Variety Orchestra*.

See Index of Composers, also pages 58–62, 80–84

Klaus Act

Yet to turn 30, Klaus Mäkelä has already risen to the highest rank of international conductors, with top jobs in Oslo, Paris, Amsterdam and Chicago. He conducts two Proms with the Royal Concertgebouw Orchestra, taking in Mozart, Mahler, Bartók, Prokofiev and anniversary-composer Berio. Other prestigious visiting orchestras this season include the Budapest Festival Orchestra, Danish National Symphony Orchestra, Leipzig Gewandhaus Orchestra, Melbourne Symphony Orchestra and Vienna Philharmonic.

23 & 24 AUGUST *(See also Index of Artists)*

Contents

Concert
Orchestra

National
Orchestra
& Chorus
of Wales

Philharmonic
Orchestra

Scottish
Symphony
Orchestra

Singers

Symphony
Orchestra
& Chorus

BBC ORCHESTRAS & CHOIRS

Music to keep you on the edge of your seat
Music to bring you to your feet
Music for everyone, everywhere, live and on air

bbc.co.uk/orchestras

iPLAYER SOUNDS

The Proms

Poet Laureate **SIMON ARMITAGE** pays tribute to the
Proms audience, whose expectation and captivation
he says 'are as much part of the music as the notes'

A London evening leaves its hustle and hassle outside,
enters the hushed dome, the upholstered dark.
Here comes the soft percussion of footsteps wandering
    down to the front,
the fluted burble of small-talk and chat.
The air in the hall seems tuned to the wavelength of songs,
every box, alcove and arch is an ear cupped for what
    happens next.

So the violin gathers its thoughts.
And the oboe holds its breath.
And the trombone strains at the bit.
And the piccolo bites its lip.
And the bass drum slows its pulse to a dead stop
until the conductor touches the tip of a wand to the
    sweet-spot of silence
and something called music begins.

Look how music falls like light on the faces of strangers.
See how the harp is a heart, how the cello is human in
    body and mind.
Music – its own gravity, bending the natural laws.
Music as all time and no time at all:
in the split-second gap between sound being made
    and sound being heard
eternity hangs.

Audience, you are the instrument,
you are the tune:
a moment's pause after the final note
then all your hands are suddenly playing
the music we call applause.

HARMONY HILL

A SHORT STORY BY
LUCY CALDWELL

ILLUSTRATIONS BY
KEI-ELLA LOEWE

You stow your violin carefully in the corner of the opposite overhead locker, where you can keep an eye on it until boarding is complete – in case another passenger, or even an air steward, turns it on its side in order to heave their own suitcase in, or takes it out and shoves it in again upside down. It is a relief when the lockers are closed for take-off and you can relax a little. People think the jet-setting life of a musician must be glamorous but a lot of the time it's economy flights at unholy hours, budget hotel rooms and pre-packaged sandwiches.

Not, you think, that you're complaining. This is the life you wanted since the day you got your first quarter-sized Skylark violin – its glossy bright-red varnish, the curve of its scroll and its liquorice pegs; its shiny black case with a space for the bow and a compartment in which to keep a perfect translucent lozenge of amber rosin – with its warm, sweet, spicy smell – in a cloth in a box. You would only have

been 5 but you remember how it felt to stroke your bow over the rosin to create a puff of sticky dust, then to attach the grips of the shoulder rest to the underside of the violin, raise it to your shoulder and fit it under your chin – then to lift your bowing arm, thumb tucked into the corner of the frog, and to draw the bow across the open strings, 'A-A-A-A A, A, E-E-E-E E, E', the first notes of the 'Twinkle' variations.

These days your violin is a Peter Guarnerius, from around 1690. Well, you think of it as yours, but it's not, of course – it belongs to the Stradivari Trust and at best you are a brief custodian, a couple of bars' worth of music in its life. Long after you've had to return it to them, long after you're gone, the violin will still be played, by musicians as unimaginable to you as you must have been to Pietro of Mantua as he sat in his workshop, shaving and planing and sanding and gluing those finest cuts of flamed maple, stroking

them with his signature golden varnish in the clear light of a Lombardy evening.

At the airport this evening they subjected your case, as they almost always do, to an extra scan. As the airport security officer tugged at the neck strap and yanked the violin out you had to stop yourself from yelling – that the instrument she was spinning round one-handedly, holding up to squint through the f-holes, careless, bored, was older than all of this – older than the airport, older than the invention of aviation. Older than the USA itself.

But you know by now that you have to be polite – that, in practice, airport staff hold all the power. You still have nightmares about the budget airline that insisted your flight was overbooked and that you'd have to put the violin in the cargo hold – where it could have been jounced around, where the extreme cold could have irrevocably damaged it – even as you showed them proof of the extra seat that you had paid for just to make sure it could travel onboard with you. You were on your way to Ljubljana in that instance and had to miss the competition rather than risk the violin's life. This evening you just had to stand there as the security officer dumped your bows ignominiously into a dirty plastic tray and onto the X-ray belt to be shunted along beside people's carry-on bags and a fold-up buggy. Sorry, you'd thought to your bows, forgive me … Ask any string musician and they'll likely admit to feeling as protective of their bows as their instrument – maybe more so. At least, you think, you're not travelling with a cello.

You've been here in North Carolina for a week-long festival of Irish-Appalachian music. There are deep Ulster-Scots connections in this part of the world – the Presbyterian lowland Scots who fled the persecution of both the native Irish and the ruling English; the Highland Scots defeated at Culloden, as well as the Irish who fled the Famine and survived the coffin ships, many of them settling in the foothills of the Blue Ridge Mountains with their fiddles and flutes and pipes.

Your own programme here has been fun, built around showcasing contemporary Irish composers, with quartets by Elaine Agnew and Jane O'Leary, *Ready-Steady-Go!* and *Forever begin …*, alongside the Beethoven your quartet is renowned for, in this instance his mysterious, transcendent No. 14 in C sharp minor, reputedly his own favourite; and the *Grosse Fuge*, that immense quartet condemned by contemporary critics,

but which Stravinsky declared 'an absolutely contemporary piece of music that will be contemporary forever'. You remember the first time you heard it yourself, as a teenager, when it came on the car radio; trying to work out if it was Bartók or Hindemith, or maybe even Stravinsky – the shock when the announcer revealed it was Beethoven! You think that's where your fascination with him began – his Romance No. 2 had been the first piece you fell in love with, your own first proper solo piece, sweet and vibrato-laden, but here was something entirely unexpected – disturbing, stirring, new. He'd been deaf for a whole decade by the time he wrote it, and you think of him, tormented – those awful, pleading, angry letters he wrote to his beloved nephew Karl – trying to capture the sounds he would never hear played. How strange it is, you think, that 200 years later people's whole lives would be devoted to that music. For the 21 years of your professional life, yours has been.

The air stewards are giving the safety demonstration – they're at the part where in the event of an evacuation you must leave all personal possessions behind. No way, you say back to them silently. In the event of an evacuation or a forced landing on water your violin is coming with you. When they ask you to check your nearest emergency exit, you factor in the steps it would take to get to the overhead locker first. Then you picture yourself treading water in the darkly roiling Atlantic Ocean, holding the silver case above your head as a mother might an infant.

Now the stewards are walking the aisles, checking seatbelts and mobile devices. You look at your phone one last time. Lami (hopefully with cello) has flown back to London to see her husband and daughter but Jonny and Aidan have stayed on for a couple of days' holiday in Nashville – the group chat today has been full of pictures of them trying on Stetsons and studded cowboy boots, and just this evening the two of them grinning alongside charred racks of ribs as long as their forearms.

'Oh yeah,' the pictures are captioned. 'Going in. Bet Morag wishes she was here.'

'Gross!' you text, and for emphasis the green boking face – you're vegetarian.

People think it must be romantic making music so intensely together, all heartache and torrid affairs. Really it's just like having permanent siblings.

'Flight on time?' Aidan texts, and you give the thumbs up.

'Hope no babies!' he texts. On the flight over you and he were seated beside a baby who cried in minor seconds almost the entire way. You glance around – you've been so focused on your violin, it hasn't occurred to you to check. Fortunately it seems to be only adults nearby.

'Friendly reminder folks, make sure you come in on Monday with the bluegrass nailed,' texts Jonny.

You turn off your phone and exhale. You're flying back to Dublin then going straight on up to Belfast to give a masterclass to the School of Music's top youth quartets, before flying back to London the next morning for the final rehearsals ahead of the first of your own quartet's autumn concert series.

It's pretty brutal, your schedule, you think ruefully. You'll be going straight from the airport to the Aircoach, and pretty much straight from the bus stop to the Harty Room, where the masterclass is to be held. Your parents live 40 minutes' drive out of the city centre, too far to get there and back. You've booked a room at the Europa, right by the bus stop, in the hope that you can get an early check-in, dump your bag and have a quick shower. It's not ideal, turning up jet-lagged, straight off a red-eye, off the back of a week-long series of performances. But you owe the School of Music so much – from those very first days of the Junior Strings, up through the Training Strings to the City of Belfast Youth Orchestra, it was your life. Your first ever tours were with those youth orchestras – to the Béla Bartók Concert Hall in Budapest, to Fiesole in Italy, where you played in an amphitheatre at dusk, to the great chestnut dome of Boston's riverside Hatch Shell, to Washington DC and the White House. The conductors, the section tutors, who gave it their all; who told you that you were, or could be, world-class musicians, no matter who you were or where you came from. You remember the masterclass you took, aged 15, with Tasmin Little on Elgar's Violin Concerto, how much it meant that she was there, that *Tasmin Little* was in Belfast. How star-struck all of you were by how

glamorous she was, the dangly emerald earrings that danced as she played …

Well, you can't compete with Tasmin Little on the glamour front. You are the second violin in a respected, prize-winning quartet that has played in dozens of cities all over the globe. You're not a soloist, though – you're not a concert violinist. You used to think that you, too, would one day walk on stage to play with, say, the Berlin Philharmonic, in a strapless ball dress and earrings, to the sweeping bow of the conductor.

But when you walk into the Harty Room tomorrow with your Peter Guarnerius, your Lafleur bow, fresh from America, bound for the Wigmore Hall, you will represent more than most of them could dream of. You would never renege on them. It's your duty to play it forwards.

The School of Music has asked you to explore with the youth quartets what it means to play Beethoven – what the secret to him is. You have no idea, yet, what you should say. What would you say to your childhood self, if you could? What might your childhood self say back?

As soon as the plane is safely airborne you recline your seat, put on your padded eye-mask. You rarely manage to sleep on flights, but there is a comfort in going through familiar scores in your head, the absorbing complexities of them. You're trying to learn Mark O'Connor's 'Bluegrass' String Quartet in time to add it to the repertoire for your upcoming concerts. After you heard him play in the festival's gala opening concert, a virtuosic

performance that brought down the house, Jonny got hold of the sheet music, saying it would pair perfectly with Beethoven's String Quartet No. 11 in F minor, the 'Serioso' – the rage of the opening Allegro con brio, the way the first violin leaps about so wildly in octaves, the seething semiquaver runs. But you don't yet know the 'Bluegrass' well enough by heart to run it now. You know your own part, but it's not about that – you need to know all of the parts, to be able to play them simultaneously in your head. You'll have to study the score on the coach, you think. And in the meantime you still have to work out what to say about Beethoven.

There's a moment you sometimes get after several hours of rehearsals, when things have fallen apart, and you've been battling them, and battling each other, and in your despair you give up, and that's the moment they start to fit together again. You try to give yourself over to it now – that same sense of surrender.

The aeroplane roars on through the weightless night and you're not yet 4 years old, your favourite toy the music set that packs up inside a green plastic drum. You dig your fingers under the thick yellow lid to prise it off and inside are a pair of cymbals, shiny red castanets, some sleigh-bells, a tambourine and a pair of smooth wooden drumsticks – you hook the handle of the sleigh-bells around your foot and sling the tambourine around your arm, put the lid of the drum back on and hang the strap round your neck and march around beating it, jangling with every step, your sister toddling behind

clashing the cymbals. Your mother is heavily pregnant with the baby who will any day now be your new baby sister, and after lunch you all curl up together on your mum's bed and she puts on her cassette tape of Jacqueline du Pré. The first piece is Mendelssohn's *Song without Words*, and as it plays you lie there rapt, listening to the cello swooping and dipping and spiralling up, and you say that you want to make music like *that*. You say it often enough that your mother starts to think maybe music lessons would be a good idea – something to occupy you, when any day now she'll have three wains under 4. In the phone book she finds a teacher of the Suzuki Method, which takes children from a very young age. It's not the cello, but the closest she can find, the violin, and the following spring you start going on Saturday mornings to a group lesson in a place called, as if in a fairy tale, Harmony Hill. At first you sit cross-legged at the back of the room while a semi-circle of children and their parents play the 'Twinkle' Variations, 'Lightly Row', 'Song of the Wind', 'Go Tell Aunt Rhody' …

From the beginning you are entranced. After a few weeks of going on Saturdays, you and your sister get your first violins – not the quarter-sized Skylark you will be so proud of, but a 'violin' made by the music teacher's husband from an empty chocolate box, with the inner tube of a kitchen roll for a neck and coloured dots where your fingers go; and for a bow there is a length of bamboo. Your dad laughs at your chocolate-box violins, and at the sturdy one made for your baby sister,

from the green box that contained her first baby shoes, says if these are music lessons, your mum's being taken for a ride. But there is a logic to it – they weigh next to nothing, so they're comfortable to hold; they don't break if you drop or sit or stand on them, or if they do then it doesn't matter; and they let you concentrate on posture and rhythm, on basic technique, without having to worry about the sound, because any sound you make at first is likely to be awful, a scraping, sawing, squeaking noise that would put anyone off. So for months you play and play on your chocolate box, 'Oh Come, Little Children', 'May Song', 'Long, Long Ago'; you match your bow strokes to the other children's and your fingers to the dots matching notes the teacher calls out, 'Open A, Open A, A1, A2, A2, A3, Open E, E1, Open E, A3 …' and you long for the day you are deemed worthy of your first real violin. It is one of the tenets of Suzuki that the parent has to learn the instrument too, and so when you and your sister get your first Skylarks your mum gets one too, and so that she doesn't feel left out, so does your youngest sister, an eighth-sized model that looks like something a doll would play. Every evening after dinner your mum pushes back the kitchen table and the four of you play, and your dad makes his daily joke about how he preferred it when you were the chocolate-box quartet. He might be tone deaf, he says, but in his opinion the music sounded better when it was imaginary.

What happened to your chocolate-box violin? Discarded as soon as you got your

Skylark, of course, and consigned without fanfare to the toy box, or given back to the teacher for another beginner. You haven't thought of it for years, but it's still there inside of you somewhere – the faint sweet smell of it, sugar, cardboard and glue, and the silver stars, one for every group lesson, that you stick on the sides until it glitters with its own private magic as you sway.

Another thing happens that autumn – Jacqueline du Pré dies. Your mum plays her cassette tape over and over and cries, though she says it isn't because du Pré has died, it's for the moment she realised her fingers could undo the clasps of her cello case no longer; it's for the cancelled concerts; for the music unplayed. But the music, your violin teacher says, is still there, not just because we have recordings of it but because every note ever played is still somewhere, going up and out and on through the universe … Which is why, she says, we must take care to make the most beautiful sounds we can, not just in our music but in our everyday life, and especially in our everyday life; because either way, harmonious or discordant, it will all be there forever, and it will be what survives of us, our contribution to eternity –

You are jolted out of it. Suddenly somehow the hours of the flight have passed, and the air steward is tapping you on the shoulder and asking you to raise the blind and put your seat-back upright, and the air is thick with the metallic smell of reheated sausages and eggs from the breakfast service. You blink and wince as the sharp daylight streams in, and try to hold on to something of the feeling you had, the place you were, but it's gone.

The plane lands, taxis to its stand and the seatbelt sign pings off. You retrieve your violin and secure it on your back, contorting your stiff shoulders to wriggle each arm through. To have survived three and a half centuries, all of the wars that swept through Europe in the 18th and 19th and 20th centuries, to have stayed intact in all the hands through which it's passed, to have made it multiple times through 21st-century airport security … It's a truism, of course, that music unites us – but yet there is an unfathomable truth to it. Most mysterious of all, you think, are the ways that we're united not just across the world, Ireland to Appalachia, West to Middle East, but down through time and out into the future, some divine accordionist stretching and collapsing and extending us again.

Through Arrivals now, and baggage reclaim, and out into the damp grey Dublin morning, through the smokers and the vapers and the shopping centre to the bus stop, and onto the coach to Belfast. The seat beside you is free, and you strap your violin in.

The thing you'll have to find a way of telling the students about Beethoven, you think, turning it over in your head as the coach settles into its speed on the motorway, is that he isn't actually that technically difficult, not even in the late quartets, not really. They won't believe that, of course, but you'll have to convey to them that it's really all about how you blend, and *that's* about, yes, knowing the music and knowing each other, the hours you've spent together, in practice and performance, but even more than any of that it's how you must learn to hear the music in your head the moment before it's played. Beethoven could, you'll tell them – maybe that's what we could call his secret. That the music truly starts in the silence before, the silence that calls it, through longing, into being. They have to listen for it with all of their bodies and all of their senses, but with their imaginations too. Yes, you think. Something like that.

The 'Bluegrass' score is on your lap. You'll open it in just a minute. But now you lean your head against the window, close your eyes. The feeling wells up in you of lying in bed at night as a child, listening to the tape recorder – 'The Happy Farmer' and 'Gavotte'; goodness, you think, you haven't thought of those pieces in years. For a moment you can hear the skips and hops, the sadder bit, the pizzicato, and you remember the way you used to think of each and every one of those notes dancing up through the ceiling and out through the rooftop and upwards into the sky, through the flickering leaves of the birch tree, through the chopping blades of helicopters and up through the clouds, into the stratosphere, until the hiss and the click came of the end of the tape. ●

Lucy Caldwell is a Belfast-born author of four novels and three collections of short stories. She is a Fellow of the Royal Society of Literature and her honours include the E. M. Forster Award from the American Academy of Arts & Letters. She grew up playing the violin and was a member of the City of Belfast Youth Orchestra.

Kei-Ella Loewe is a South African illustrator based in the Netherlands. Self-taught, she works mainly as a book-cover artist, and likes to create art that is dreamy, emotive and feminine.

I Wonder as I Wander

MICHAEL SPITZER ventures along the byways that connect music with movement, landscape and the seasons. Can examining the three compass points of listening, performing and creating alter the course of our own musical journeys?

The *Dawn of Everything*, a remarkable book by a pair of anthropologists, David Graeber and David Wengrow, noted that many cultures swing between opposite social systems across their year. Over the summer hunting season Inuit society is highly authoritarian, becoming more democratic and altruistic during winter, when the Inuit shelter together against the harsh arctic environment. Listening to my favourite Christmas carol last December ('In the Bleak Midwinter', to Gustav Holst's tune), I was struck by how Britain's two main music festivals also pull us in opposite directions. Christmas is a feast not just of food and drink but of the songs and carols we love. It is a time of hunkering down indoors with family and friends, an intimacy the Danes call *hygge* and the Germans *Gemütlichkeit*, to take comfort in the pleasures of familiarity. In musical terms this means enjoying sheer repetition. During the Covid-19 lockdowns, Spotify downloads of classic songs far outstripped those of the latest hits. At times of crisis we hug the familiar.

Now consider all the ways that the Proms, the UK's great summer festival, takes us along new paths. Summer is a season not of sheltering but of travelling, and Pierre Boulez did well to wonder at the 'eccentricity of London to have that much audience during the summer', when Parisians tend to flee their capital. Unlike the intimacy of a carol, a Proms concert is a mass coming together of a crowd of strangers, united by the music.

And whereas many listeners flock to hear familiar classics such as Beethoven's 'Choral' Symphony (No. 9), the major draw of the Proms is arguably the spirit of discovery, to hear something new. The mental journey of discovering new music caps the physical journey that has got you to the Royal Albert Hall. I suggest that the idea of journeying, ultimately of walking, flows naturally from the spirit of Promming itself, that is, of listening as an aural promenade. (The title 'Proms' comes from 'Promenade Concerts', a feature of Victorian London's pleasure gardens, at which visitors were free to stroll, eat, drink and smoke.) For the philosopher Friedrich Nietzsche, 'Our first question about the value of a book, of a human being, or a musical composition is: Can it walk?'

It's hard to escape the idea that creativity in general is associated with moving. Adam Moss's *The Work of Art*, one of Barack Obama's favourite books of 2024, reports that motion or travelling is integral to the creative process of many of the artists interviewed within. The photographer Gregory Crewdson gets many of his ideas while long-distance swimming. For the visual artist Cheryl Pope, it is boxing. The playwright Tony Kushner is inspired by riding subway trains. One thinks of Stockhausen, his ear pressed attentively to airplane windows, listening to the engine sounds. A book could be written on Mahler's love of cycling. The work of the artist 'who composes while walking', according to the philosopher Frédéric Gros, 'retains and expresses the energy, the springiness of the body'.

One also remembers music history's most famous walker, Beethoven, sketching in the fields outside Vienna. After his morning walk, he would return to the quiet of his study to contemplate his sketches. Opinion is divided on whether the three activities of walking, thinking and listening help or hinder each other. It's complex. On the one hand, the great 17th-century French polymath Marin Mersenne, like Plato before him, rejected impassioned music as a distraction from the contemplative life. On the other hand, my daily walks with my dog wouldn't be complete without my wireless headphones. Listening while walking helps me think.

This is by no means to discount the effect of standing still. Might it be this act, practised by a portion of the audience at each Prom in the Royal Albert Hall, that led the festival's founder-conductor Henry Wood to remark to the audience during a wartime Last Night: 'I am amazed by your stillness and how you listen'? The concert etiquette of still, quiet listening may not be unique to the West (North Indian classical music espouses it), but it certainly dominates our listening behaviour. Many of history's greatest writers, including Dickens, Hemingway and Churchill, wrote standing up. Writing while standing improves blood flow and sharpens concentration. This makes sense for evolutionary reasons, because standing (upright bipedal stance) is the optimal posture humans use to interact with their environment, especially music.

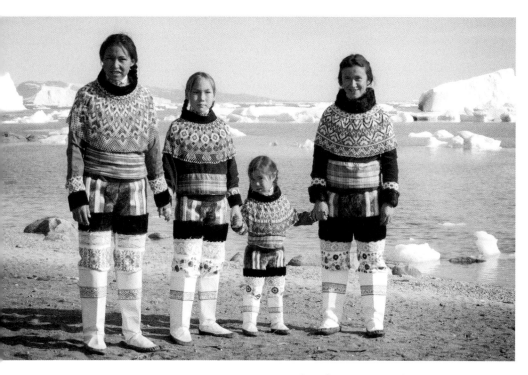

Inuit people standing on the shores of Disko Bay, western Greenland; the contrast in their societal behaviours and customs between winter and summer is echoed by that of our own 'seasonal' musical needs, which determine whether we hunker down with the familiar or go exploring the new

Standing permits what psychologists call 'full-body entrainment'; *ie*, moving with the beat with every limb. It's hard, if not impossible, to dance in your seat.

So what is to be gained from standing at a Proms concert, or from just sitting still? We are better able to attend to how the music moves. In the words of the painter Paul Klee, the music 'takes a line for a walk'. Composer Harrison Birtwistle was much taken by Klee's phrase, as he was by Klee's notion of an 'imaginary landscape'. In his *Silbury Air* for chamber orchestra, Birtwistle takes a musical line for a walk around Silbury Hill, a prehistoric mound in Wiltshire, presenting shifting perspectives on the hill in the changing light. The idea of music as a 'landscape'

through which we 'walk' isn't an idiosyncratic metaphor. It has been baked into the evolution of our species ever since our earliest hominin ancestors got up on their hind legs 4.4 million years ago. Simply by walking, Australopithecines triggered a process by which the brain's auditory and motor cortexes, responsible respectively for hearing and motion, began to knit together. This is why all kinds of physical movement, from gestures to dance steps to walking itself, are inseparable from our experience of music. And, thanks to mirror neurons in our brain that detect motion, we identify with musical motion in much the same way that we mirror body language in others. While Western music is saturated with dances, marches and processions, in the rest of the world, music is often grounded in physical landscapes. The Aboriginal peoples of Australia thread their songlines as they walk through the desert en route to communal gatherings in the dry season. The intertwined melodies of the Bayaka Pygmies of Cameroon reflect the criss-crossing animal trails that they track through the forest. On receiving his first bull, a boy from the Dinka in South Sudan, a cattle culture, will follow it around in the field singing to it for many hours. Back in the West, cattle even roam Beethoven's imaginary landscape, lifted, as it were, to the sky of musical abstraction. In the finale of his 'Pastoral' Symphony (No. 6), an Alpine horn summons a procession of cows down a mountain, addressed by a traditional Swiss herding tune, or *ranz de vaches*.

You only appreciate this if you know the Alpine tradition. As with real landscapes, navigating imaginary ones is rewarded by expert knowledge. If you know what to look for, a landscape can be read. The wonderful books by the natural navigator Tristan Gooley teach us that, when the leaves on a tree are bisected by a strong pale line, this is a sign that there is water nearby. The exposed rock in a mountainside is angled up towards the south and down towards the north. Puddles on east–west paths look different from those on north–south paths because of the angle of evaporation. By the same principle, experienced listeners navigate the landmarks of sonata form. They might recognise a development section from the speed of harmonic change, and know that a retransition signals impending return to the home key. They may know that Mahler's orchestral waves come in cumulative groups of three. They may be aware that, in middle-period Ligeti, the halfway point is signposted when the micropolyphony (dense array of overlapping individual lines) momentarily coalesces around the specific interval of a tritone played in octaves. Our path around the musical Silbury Hill is illuminated when we learn that Birtwistle liked to rotate static harmonic blocks. It's no coincidence that the first guides to Wagner's leitmotifs (musical themes or fragments that signify a particular character or idea) mimicked the popular Baedeker travel guides of the 1860s. Given our deference to geographers, why are we still so sniffy about musical knowledge, including the

We're All in it Together

The changing dialogue – over times and cultures – between performer and listener

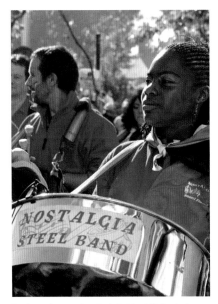

Steelpan players at London's Notting Hill Carnival: typically the audience gets involved through dancing

When a Trinidadian steelpan band plays a calypso, audience members dance in their seats and join in by playing irons, drums and gourds (scratchers), traditional percussion instruments. At a concert of North Indian classical music, audiences respond with gestures and comments. Indeed, the musicians value such instant feedback, because they view the event as being constituted by all the participants, not just the players. Such 'participatory' behaviour is common in musics as wide apart as the Shona of Zimbabwe, the Peruvian Aymara, American bluegrass and the chants of football stadiums, where the performers and the listeners are the same people. Most cultures don't separate music from dancing, so even dancing to songs in a Western music festival is a way of participating. All this is a long way from the etiquette of Western classical

concerts, where there is a sort of 'iron curtain' between performers and listeners that originates in the Ancient Greek meaning of 'orchestra' as a space marked off from the theatre audience. It is fair to say that most listeners in the West today consume their music passively through still, quiet listening to recordings instead of being actively engaged with live music as composers and performers. This is a shame because, despite our ideology that musicians are exceptional creatures with a God-given talent, everyone is born with a capacity to be musical. Neuroscience teaches us that oxytocin – a hormone involved in musical pleasure – is increased when we listen in groups rather than alone, and that playing music engages more of the brain than just listening. It is tempting, then, to view music history in the West as a downward spiral, from a 'participatory' golden age to our modern era of lonely, passive listening. Fortunately, this isn't entirely true.

With easily available music production software such as Soundtrap, GarageBand and Reason (a Digital Audio Workstation), it's never been easier for people who can't play an instrument or read staff notation to make music. As a tool rather than a threat, AI will work to further 'democratise' music, allowing everyone to get involved if they so wish. But even the act of listening to music in your armchair through earbuds isn't as passive or lonely as it might seem. Listening plugs you into a social network, because all music is made up of conventional patterns. Moreover, attending to music critically and with imagination, rather than merely enjoying 'the sound it makes' (as the conductor Thomas Beecham unkindly accused the British of doing!), is an activity. Personally, I find that being pinned down to my seat at a classical music concert makes me listen all the more actively. Still and silent as I am, I am fully participating.

Michael Spitzer

'How happy I am to be able to walk among the shrubs, the trees, the woods, the grass and the rocks! For the woods, the trees and the rocks give man the resonance he needs': Beethoven on one of his many walks in the countryside (painting by Julius Schmid, 1854–1935)

Proms's abiding ethos stemming from the BBC's mission, laid down by its first Director-General, Lord Reith, to 'inform, educate and entertain'?

Perhaps it's cooler to think of musical learning as a kind of mountaineering, blending walking with strenuous, gravity-defying climbing, and ultimately with the exaltation afforded by great heights. This is why one of the most influential contrapuntal treatises of all time, by the 18th-century pedagogue Johann Fux, is called *Gradus ad Parnassum* ('Steps up Mount Parnassus'), and why mountains loom large in 19th-century Romanticism, especially in the symphonies of Bruckner, Mahler and Strauss. The listener's climb, in the Adagio of Bruckner's Seventh Symphony – from the subterranean Wagner tubas of the opening to the blazing trumpet fanfares of the apotheosis – is both a spiritual journey and an ascent through the Austrian landscape. Illuminations happen on mountain tops, earned by the effort to reach them. 'I am,' says Nietzsche's Zarathustra, 'a wanderer and mountain-climber.' According to Nietzsche, we write well 'only with our feet'.

Descending from his hikes, that other intrepid musical mountaineer, Anton Webern, liked to bring back rare Alpine flowers to preserve or plant in his garden. It is a perfect analogy for where his abstraction comes from. You can hear how Webern's Symphony, Op. 21, distils the Alpine soundscape of Mahler's Ninth Symphony – the horn, harp and double bass timbres of its opening – into a rare perfume. For me, Webern is far from 'abstract'; his music is as aromatic as that of any mid-Winter festival. And yet musical mountaineering wasn't invented in the 19th century, nor in the West. How fitting that the first named composer in the history of the world, the Sumerian princess Enheduanna (2285–50 BCE), daughter of Sargon the Great, sang her hymns to the moon goddess Ishtar on top of the ziggurat of Ur. It makes sense to sing somewhere high, because that is where the gods live. Church bells and calls to prayer sound in high towers not just because they can be heard for miles, but because God is listening. Over the ages, music absorbed climbing into itself. Acoustically, notes want to rise, sometimes abetted by incense. It is the natural trajectory of Carnatic *kriti*, Hindustani *ragas*, Pakistani *qawwali*, Isolde's *Liebestod*, the songs of Van Morrison or, for that matter, most music in the world, to rise to a peak of spiritual ecstasy. As the melody climbs up to the Divine, it carries the listener with it. London isn't particularly noted for its mountains. But it has one, just off Hyde Park, a magic mountain. So, if you are lucky enough to climb a Proms concert this season to hear Errollyn Wallen's *The Elements*, Sibelius's Violin Concerto, Birtwistle's *Earth Dances* or any of the countless other works on offer, let your imagination roam. ●

Michael Spitzer is a Professor of Music at Liverpool University with an interest in how music intersects with philosophy, psychology, biology and religion. His books include *A History of Emotion in Western Music: A Thousand Years from Chant to Pop* (OUP, 2020) and *The Musical Human: A History of Life on Earth* (Bloomsbury, 2021), which was featured as a Radio 4 *Book of the Week*.

Help Musicians

Music connects us, uniting communities, bridging cultures and enriching our lives.

We've been a charity supporting professional musicians in times of crisis and opportunity for over 100 years.

A career in music remains challenging. We exist to help musicians with a broad range of support to help navigate tough economic uncertainties, maintain physical and mental wellbeing and find new ways to learn, develop and grow.

Help Musicians is extremely grateful to the Promenaders' Musical Charities for its long-standing support and commitment to our work in wanting a world where musicians thrive.

Love music? Donate today and support our work.

Registered Charity No.228089
Help Musicians is the working name of the Musicians' Benevolent Fund

Discover …

Symphony No. 2

EMMA KAVANAGH introduces a neglected French symphony that reflects the turbulence in Europe ahead of the Second World War

When the 19-year-old Elsa Barraine (1910–99) was announced as the winner of the 1929 Prix de Rome, much of the press reporting focused more on her appearance – petite, tomboyish, with a head of untamed curls – than on her music. Beneath this seemingly unassuming exterior, however, lay a determined and steely personality that would not be cowed by the gendered expectations of the time. Indeed, Barraine would rise quickly to become one of France's most influential musical figures, with an active life both in and out of the concert hall.

Born into a musical family, Barraine trained at the Paris Conservatoire and soon found an interest in composition in the classes of Paul Dukas. After winning numerous Conservatoire prizes in her teens, she was only the fourth woman to win the top spot in the Prix de Rome since the competition's inauguration in 1803. Her residency in Rome was set against a backdrop of rising Fascism in Italy, spearheaded by Benito Mussolini. On returning to Paris she pursued a career in broadcasting, working for French national radio (Radiodiffusion Française) for several years. During the Second World War she joined the French Resistance and was a founding member of the French Communist Party's Front National des Musiciens. These political activities, and her Jewish heritage, made her an obvious target for the authorities: she twice evaded capture and spent the last months of the Occupation in hiding under a false name. After the war she resumed her media work before pursuing a new path as a teacher at the Paris Conservatoire and as a theatre inspector for the Ministry of Culture. Barraine wrote little music later in life, though at her death she left over 150 compositions in a variety of genres.

Much of her music was directly inspired by the political turmoil that surrounded her, and her Symphony No. 2 (1938) – perhaps her best-known work – is no exception. Subtitled 'Voyna' ('War' in Russian), this symphony gives voice to the tension and turbulence of the late 1930s. It is not a long work – a little under 20 minutes – but the rapid changes in style and mood create a sense of unease that reflects the emotional weight of its subject matter. Though it was seldom performed during the war, Barraine's Symphony No. 2 found a firmer footing after the Liberation in 1944 – and now, thanks to tireless advocates of her music, has a new life in our concert halls today. ●

Emma Kavanagh is a musicologist and cultural historian at Aix-Marseille Université. A specialist in opera and musical culture in France between the Revolution and the First World War, she is currently working on a collaborative archival project in partnership with the Aix-en-Provence Festival.

Barraine Symphony No. 2
31 JULY

IMPERIAL

Stay close to the action

Just a five-minute walk from the Royal Albert Hall, Prince's Gardens offers great-value accommodation from July to September.

Book now

vacenquiries@imperial.ac.uk

(+44) 020 7594 3333

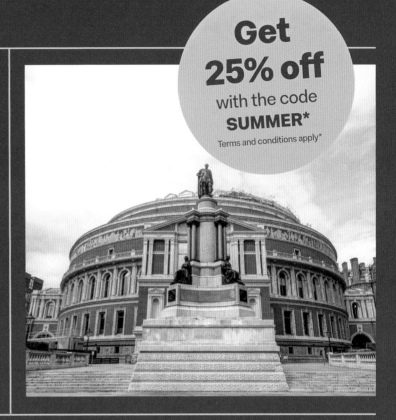

Imperial College London

imperial.ac.uk/visit/summer-accommodation

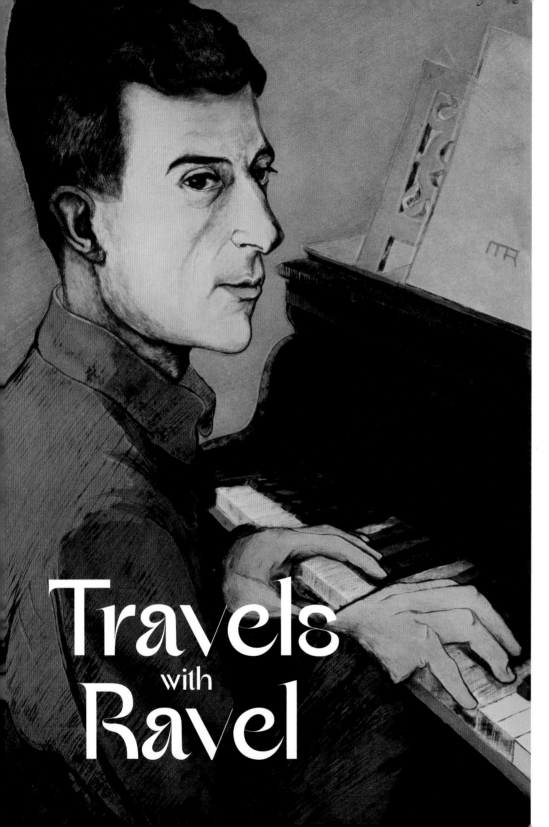

Travels
with
Ravel

Inspired equally by Spain and the Far East, by fairy tales and obsessive rhythms, Maurice Ravel – the creator of shimmering sound-worlds underpinned by meticulous detail – presented a tangle of enigmas. In the 150th-anniversary year of the great French composer's birth, **BARBARA L. KELLY** unravels them

Portrait of Ravel by Achille Ouvré (1872–1951)

Maurice Ravel was born in the Basque seaside town of Ciboure, near the French–Spanish border, 150 years ago. His music astonished and puzzled audiences and critics during his lifetime, and has continued to do so ever since. It is beautifully crafted, transports us to fantastical places and provokes a dizzying array of emotions. The effect is so alluring that it can be a struggle to discover the man behind the music. Charges of his being a conjuror, imitator and master of artifice have only added to his appeal, because we are never quite sure what is real and what is imagined.

Crossing real and imagined borders was a constant in Ravel's work. He was born to Basque/Swiss parents and lived most of his life in Paris, but his music often brings to mind disparate worlds. A number of Ravel's works are inspired by, and evoke, the Far East or Africa or Ancient Greece. His fondness for *japonisme* and *chinoiserie* rode the wave of 'exoticism' that was fashionable in turn-of-the-century France, a phenomenon that spanned literature, drama, music, art and interior design. Ravel's house at Montfort-l'Amaury, 25 miles west of Paris and now a museum, was full of replica art objects. Sometimes Ravel gives merely a hint of a particular culture he is imagining, using a combination of slightly altered scales, vibrant rhythms and orchestral colour to suggest a place. At other times it is clear that he is engaging more deeply; this is the case with some of his Spanish

settings and in his remarkably forthright *Chansons madécasses* ('Madagascan Songs', 1925–6), in which he discloses his anger towards the white oppressors of the Madagascan people.

66 Ravel's music transports us to fantastical places and provokes a dizzying array of emotions. The effect is so alluring that it can be a struggle to discover the man behind the music. 99

Shéhérazade, his cycle of three songs for voice and orchestra, provides a fascinating range of examples. It was composed in 1903 while Ravel was still studying at the Paris Conservatoire but already making his mark with Parisian audiences. The first of the songs, 'Asie', plays with the sound of its title (Asia) – turning the idea of the place into an object of desire with oboe solos and orchestral eruptions. Other words break through the musical fabric, notably 'fantasy' and 'mystery'. On closer listening, we hear the narrator's desire to travel to Damascus, Persia and China, in order to witness colourful sights and extremes of emotion and to recount their adventures upon returning home. The subsequent two songs focus more predictably on human desire. In 'La flûte enchantée' (The Enchanted Flute) a servant hears her lover (represented by a rhapsodic

flute) beneath her window. In 'L'Indifférent' (The Indifferent One) we encounter what appears to be a same-sex desire for a youthful stranger, who remains indifferent and remote. This was a rare instance of Ravel addressing the then controversial subject of homosexuality – a subject that, some have thought, reflected his own inclination.

Spain was a journey closer to home – Ravel's mother was Basque and had lived in Madrid – and he was attracted to the country's sights and sounds throughout his creative life, from the early solo-piano 'Habanera' (one of the two *Sites auriculaires* for piano, 1895) to the *Don Quixote* songs (1932–3).

Ravel's *Rapsodie espagnole* was begun during his 'Spanish' year of 1907 (alongside the Toledo-set opera *L'heure espagnole* and the *Vocalise-étude en forme de habanera*). This substantial orchestral work has a wide expressive range. The first of its four movements, 'Prélude à la nuit', starts with a murmur and remains subdued. Gradually we hear gentle Spanish rhythms in the voluptuous strings and finally in more insistent wind and brass interjections. Although Ravel's predecessors Chabrier and Rimsky-Korsakov are discernibly part of the *Rapsodie*'s 'Spanish' heritage, we get a hint, too, of the future: the clarinet duo prefigures the sound of the lovelorn puppet at the centre of Stravinsky's ballet *Petrushka* (1911).

The *Rapsodie*'s other three movements – 'Malagueña', 'Habanera' (both Spanish

although they have also thrived in the concert hall. Ravel, as one of the most innovative French composers, caught the attention of the influential impresario Serge Diaghilev of the Ballets Russes company. *Daphnis and Chloe* was Ravel's only commission from Diaghilev and was produced in collaboration with choreographer Mikhail Fokine and designer Léon Bakst. Ravel's musical depiction of innocence and awakening desire in an imagined ancient Greece resulted in one of his most sumptuous scores, which starts from almost nothing and ends with an unrivalled climax for full orchestra and wordless chorus. Here his imagination could have full rein because one could only dream of travelling to ancient Greece.

This was not the case with his next, abortive Diaghilev commission – *La valse*. Ravel's subject, the Viennese waltz, had been on his mind since 1906, but the work was only realised after the collapse of the Austro-Hungarian Empire following the First World War. Fellow composer Francis Poulenc recalled being at the famous meeting when Ravel was invited to play through the score in front of a few musicians, including Stravinsky. Diaghilev's response caused a rift between the two men: 'It's a masterpiece …,' the impresario declared, 'but it's not a ballet … It's the portrait of a ballet … It's the painting of a ballet.' Poulenc was struck by Ravel's dignity as he silently took his score and left. Diaghilev was reflecting critical opinion around Ravel's ability to imitate, to create

dances) and 'Feria' (Festival) take us to much more recognisable Spanish territories, in terms of both orchestral colour and dance rhythms. There are clear moments of exuberance, but Ravel's obsessive side is also evident, particularly in the 'Habanera' (an orchestration of his earlier piano piece, which was the inspiration for Debussy's 'Soirée dans Grenade' from the piano suite *Estampes*). The *Rapsodie espagnole* also looks forward to the hugely popular *Boléro*.

Ravel's fascination for dance and ballet went well beyond Spain. A number of his works were either composed as ballets or adapted afterwards. *Daphnis and Chloe* (1909–12), *La valse* (1919–20) and *Boléro* (1928) were conceived as ballets,

Set design by Léon Bakst for Ravel's ballet *Daphnis and Chloe*, whose action takes place on the pastoral island idyll of Lesbos; rather than aim for an authentic replication of Greek antiquity, Ravel was inspired by 'the Greece of my dreams'

perfectly crafted replicas rather than something more personal and creative. He was also astute in recognising that the work was out of step with the post-war artistic fashion for a stripped-back style. Critics have struggled to understand *La valse*, some seeing it as the dark reflection of a broken post-war Europe. Ravel himself described it as the 'apotheosis of the Viennese waltz' and a 'fantastical, fatal whirling'. The ballet is carefully constructed as a continuous series of waltzes and organised into two giant crescendos – the second of which concludes in total collapse. While we can recognise a pattern in Ravel's tendency to push his musical material to an extreme (we hear the same obsessiveness in *Boléro*), what is more striking is how old-fashioned the work seemed in post-war avant-garde circles alongside the starkness of Stravinsky's *Pulcinella* (1919–20) and *Symphonies of Wind Instruments* (1920), not to mention Ravel's own Sonata for Violin and Cello (1920–22). Ravel appeared to have opted out of the avant-garde, at least when he felt like it. *La valse* was first performed as an orchestral work in 1920 and only received a ballet premiere in 1929, by the company headed by the eccentric Ida Rubinstein.

Ravel's creative facility dramatically decreased after his experience of war and the loss of his mother in 1917. He suffered from various conditions that affected his sleep and made the task of composing more challenging. In 1921 he moved out of Paris to Montfort-l'Amaury. The retreat was also symbolic; Ravel chose

Redefining 'Daphnis'

John Wilson on the ballet that he conducts at the Proms, and sees as Ravel's masterpiece

Daphnis and Chloe is a piece I've been obsessed with since I was aged 18. I still have my first score of it, which I bought at J. G. Windows's music shop in Newcastle (sadly recently closed, having opened in 1908). Even at that age I realised that the piece is not only Ravel's greatest achievement – it's without doubt his masterpiece – but it also presents pretty well the pinnacle of what was then achievable with the modern orchestra. Ravel used his instruments with such imagination and skill, demonstrating his complete mastery of orchestral form – it's really quite staggering for 1912!

Before recording *Daphnis and Chloe* with the Sinfonia of London, I realised I needed to make a new editon of it – there were so many mistakes in the published score – and so I had to look at all the manuscript sources and examine them in the most forensic detail, comparing them against the published edition. When stripping the score back to its barest components, what strikes you is the economy of the material. Ravel in fact uses a very small number of ideas, but it's the way he builds structures from this limited number of ideas, and the

way he connects them together that gives the piece its overall symphonic coherence – he called it a 'choreographic symphony' even though it was intended as a ballet.

There are very few composers with an orchestral imagination like Ravel's. He uses a treasure trove of tricks and devices to create stunning effects: like the strings being divided into many parts almost throughout and the use of a wordless choir to add an other-worldly dimension. There's the offstage instruments, plus an encyclopedic knowledge of harp-writing, and a death-defying solo for the French horn.

Then there's the famous, ravishing dawn music – one of the most difficult things that orchestral woodwind players will ever face. (One of Ravel's friends quipped that it was ironic that this was written by a man who never got up before 11.15am!) Here, Ravel was pushing the players to their limits, and he achieves a sort of transcendental ecstasy. It may appear effortless on the surface but – like a swan gliding on the water's surface with its legs paddling furiously beneath – it takes a great deal of precision and technical ingenuity for that sort of effortlessness to happen.

And then there's the closing 'Danse générale' with 10 percussionists. It definitely owes a debt of gratitude to Rimsky-Korsakov, and there's a kind of orgiastic build-up to the end, which is one of the great tours de force of the repertoire. It's just thrilling – there's nothing like it.

Intriguingly, there's also something about Ravel's music that gives the impression of his being at one remove. You rarely glimpse the real Ravel, into his soul. He himself claimed that the artificial was much more preferable to the real. The surface is scintillating but he hides behind its facade.

The pianist Marguerite Long (1874–1966), who gave the premiere of Ravel's Piano Concerto in G major, once the composer had accepted that the piano part was beyond his abilities; after Long confided in Ravel that she was worried about sustaining the expansive melody of the second movement, the composer replied, 'That flowing phrase! How I worked on it day by day! It nearly killed me!'

when to visit the city and socialise, just as he chose when to engage with the latest musical fashions.

Throughout his career Ravel tended to give his works descriptive rather than genre-based titles such as symphony or concerto. This changed a little in the post-war period, with sonatas sitting alongside his ballets, songs and operas. However, it wasn't until the late 1920s that he began work on traditional symphonic forms, notably the concerto (and not one, but two simultaneously). In 1928 Ravel spoke of writing a piano concerto that he planned to take on a world tour. However, progress was interrupted when he met the pianist Paul Wittgenstein, who had lost his right arm during the war and was commissioning composers to write works for the left hand alone *(see also 'On the Other Hand', pages 30–32)*. Thus, Ravel juggled two concertos with similar deadlines, and with premieres within two weeks of each other in January 1932.

The two works inhabit very different musical worlds, although both betray Ravel's recent interest in jazz. The Piano Concerto for the Left Hand is the weightier work. Challenging himself to create 'a texture no thinner than that of a part written for both hands', Ravel wrote a virtuosic piano part that, in dialogue with the orchestra, encompasses a vast array of emotional states.

Ravel was much more vocal about his plans for the regular (two-hand) piece – the Piano Concerto in G major. While many European orchestra conductors expected

Ravel himself to perform the piano solo, the composer – aware of his diminishing abilities – was content to secure the services of the virtuoso Marguerite Long. In contrast to the left-hand concerto, this work is light and nostalgic. The first movement recalls Stravinsky's early ballets, albeit with a hint of Gershwin. In the heart-rending slow movement we hear an effortless fusion of Mozart and Saint-Saëns, but coloured by the enigmatic Satie. The finale reflects the energetic playfulness of his earlier writing. It may avoid the seriousness expected of a traditional concerto but we hear Ravel's own musical sound-world hurtle past as he takes us on a musical journey that was almost his last. ●

Barbara L. Kelly is a musicologist specialising in early 20th-century French music. She has published extensively on Ravel, Debussy, the group known as Les Six, music and conflict, and women in music. She is Head of the School of Music at the University of Leeds and immediate Past President of the Royal Musical Association.

Piano Concerto for the Left Hand
20 JULY

Rapsodie espagnole; La valse
23 JULY

Shéhérazade
10 AUGUST

Boléro
13 AUGUST

Piano Concerto in G major
15 AUGUST

Daphnis and Chloe
12 SEPTEMBER

RHS Flower Shows 2025

Experience a floral symphony
and compose memories
together at an
RHS Flower Show

RHS Chelsea Flower Show

TICKETS SELLING FAST

20 – 24 May

**RHS Hampton Court Palace
Garden Festival**

1 – 6 July

BOOK NOW
rhs.org.uk/shows

Ahead of his BBC Proms debut performing Ravel's Piano Concerto for the Left Hand, **NICHOLAS McCARTHY** introduces a little-known corner of the repertoire, tracing its origins from virtuoso novelty to the 20th-century masterpieces commissioned by Austrian war veteran Paul Wittgenstein

Discussions of piano works for the left hand alone are often coloured with a hint of scepticism. This corner of the repertoire is seen as a rarity – a mysterious niche comprising a handful of hidden gems for solo piano and a few celebrated concertos. For many, the conversation quickly turns to Ravel's legendary Piano Concerto for the Left Hand (1929–30). This masterwork, a favourite among pianists, has been performed by some of the world's greatest keyboard titans and holds a special place in my own output.

As a pianist born without my right hand, I take great delight in meeting anyone with even the slightest knowledge of left-hand repertoire. Even in the upper echelons of the classical music world, awareness of this unique body of work is limited. I'm often asked, 'Are there any other solo pieces or concertos for the left hand?' This question always sparks joy within me: it's a cue to share my passion for this hidden repertoire and its fascinating history.

The story begins in the early 19th century, when concert pianists were regarded as cultural superstars. Liszt, for instance, packed out European concert halls – in the same way that a modern-day icon such as Taylor Swift sells out stadiums in minutes. These virtuosos enthralled their audiences with their technical brilliance and

◄ Nicholas McCarthy, who performs Ravel's Piano Concerto for the Left Hand this season with the Bournemouth Symphony Orchestra

dramatic showmanship. And they often added an encore designed to astonish – such as performing dazzling feats of pyrotechnics using only their left hand. This deliberate irony – using the so-called 'weaker' hand to deliver a bravura display – was irresistible to concert-goers, and the spectacle would leave them in awe.

The trick lay in the aural illusion: left-hand works often create the impression of two (or even three) hands playing simultaneously, deceiving even the savviest listeners. Though the left hand tends to be weaker, its physiology gives it an advantage. In standard, two-handed piano repertoire the melody line is mostly projected in the right hand by the little finger, the weakest of the fingers. But in left-hand repertoire the melody line is projected by the thumb, the strongest digit, giving it greater clarity. (This is why there are over 3,000 works for left hand alone, yet only a few for the right-hand.) Another important element in the left-hand pianist's toolkit is the sustain pedal. This allows bass notes to remain present in the texture, creating a fuller sound, similar to that which two hands can achieve.

The development of serious left-hand repertoire beyond encores and novelty pieces, give or take a few real left-hand gems, did not occur until the 20th century, in the aftermath of the First World War. At the centre of this evolution was Paul Wittgenstein (1887–1961), whose story would forever alter the course of left-hand-alone music.

A member of the prominent Viennese Wittgenstein family, Paul was the son of a wealthy steel magnate and the brother of renowned philosopher Ludwig Wittgenstein. The family was deeply embedded in European high society, with close connections to some of the greatest names in art, music and culture. Paul was a gifted pianist who made his concert debut in 1913 to favourable reviews. But the outbreak of war would soon change his life forever.

Having enlisted into the Austro-Hungarian army, Wittgenstein was seriously injured fighting the Russian army in the Battle of Galicia, losing his right arm. This was, tragically, a common wartime injury: right-handed soldiers often suffered damage to their dominant limb during combat. Taken prisoner after the battle, Wittgenstein was moved to a Siberian camp. Here he etched out the lines of a piano keyboard in charcoal on the base of an upturned wooden crate, spending several hours a day hammering the phantom keys with his remaining hand. A visiting dignitary, upon witnessing this poignant and unusual sight, arranged for Wittgenstein to be transferred to another camp, one that boasted an old upright piano. Here Wittgenstein set to work figuring out how to play the pieces he adored – but with his left hand alone.

After being repatriated to Vienna in 1915, Wittgenstein faced the monumental challenge of reinventing himself as a one-handed pianist. With steely determination (and his family's immense

Paul Wittgenstein, the Austrian pianist who, after losing his right arm during the First World War, commissioned left-hand-only concertos from composers including Prokofiev, Richard Strauss, Britten, Korngold, Hindemith and Ravel

wealth and elite connections), he set out to build a career. He commissioned some of the most celebrated composers of the era to write works for him. These included concertos by Sergey Prokofiev, Richard Strauss, Benjamin Britten, Erich Korngold and Paul Hindemith. Among the works he commissioned, one stands out: Ravel's Piano Concerto for the Left Hand.

The concerto is a triumph of ingenuity and artistry. Though it was composed at around the same time as Ravel's other concerto, for two hands *(see also 'Travels with Ravel', pages 22–26)*, the works are poles apart – each a unique testament to the composer's mastery of orchestration and piano writing. I vividly remember hearing the left-hand concerto for the first time as a 15-year-old. I was captivated by its opening: an ominous, visceral rumble from the orchestra that gradually unfolds into a majestic theme, rising through the low growl of the instruments. All the while the pianist sits in suspense, waiting for their dramatic entrance. The tension is electric, and ice-cold nerves are required from the soloist as they prepare for their moment of brilliance.

Ravel was inspired by the play of water and often referenced our most precious resource in his compositions. *Jeux d'eau* ('Water Games', 1901) and 'Ondine' ('the water nymph') from *Gaspard de la nuit* (1908) convey this beautifully. Yet for me his most water-like musical achievement comes in the left-hand concerto's breathtaking extended cadenza, heard towards the end of

the work. Here the piano becomes a shimmering cascade, rippling and flowing with crystalline beauty before building to a powerful conclusion.

For a one-handed pianist like me, specialising in this extraordinary repertoire is a privilege, a responsibility and, at times, a real challenge. There are still preconceptions around disability and the pursuit of a career in music. As one of just a few classical soloists with a physical disability, I've had to show patience and resilience, and to develop a thicker skin, simply because I don't fit into the correct 'box'.

I hope that through my performances I can inspire the next generation of pianists to explore this remarkable music. Just as Wittgenstein blazed a trail for me, I aspire to light the way for others, ensuring that the legacy of left-hand-alone music continues to thrive. Like Wittgenstein, I have enjoyed commissioning composers, and I look forward to hearing yet-to-be-written masterworks for the left hand. I hope my work in promoting and performing this special repertoire enables other musicians with disabilities to feel that it is within their grasp to strive for a career in classical music. ●

Nicholas McCarthy is the first left-hand-alone pianist to have graduated from the Royal College of Music. He has performed with the Bournemouth Symphony, London Philharmonic, Royal Philharmonic and Ulster orchestras and has given recitals at the Queen Elizabeth Hall (London) and Vienna Konzerthaus. He is also in demand as a speaker, and recently collaborated with the ABRSM to produce the first piano syllabus for one hand.

Ravel Piano Concerto for the Left Hand

20 JULY

Be a Chorister
at Winchester Cathedral

Recruiting choristers now

Be part of one of the UK's most celebrated cathedral choirs with a tradition that spans over 900 years. The Choristers receive a world-class musical, spiritual and academic education that includes recording opportunities, performances and tours. Surrounded by a rich tradition of excellence, the Choristers discover their musical potential and develop skills which will set them up for an enriching life, creating cherished memories and forging lifelong friendships.

Generous bursaries included

Email **choirs@winchester-cathedral.org.uk** for more information

JOSEPH BOLOGNE, CHEVALIER DE SAINT-GEORGES'S

Violin Concerto in G major, Op. 8

CHRISTOPHER DINGLE reveals a concerto whose poise and restraint belie its composer's varied other talents – as fencer, boxer and marksman

How many composers or virtuoso violinists could swim across the River Seine with one arm behind their back? Or prevail against all comers in a fencing competition? Or fight off assassination attempts in Paris and London? We might well ask ourselves these questions when listening to the Violin Concerto in G major, Op. 8, by Joseph Bologne, Chevalier de Saint-Georges (1745–99), since the composer of this highly refined music did all these things, and much more besides. The reflective poise of the melancholy slow movement was crafted by a man regarded not just as the finest fencer and swordsman in Europe, but also as a peerless boxer, marksman, ice-skater, huntsman, swimmer and dancer. His biography reads like a cross between *Amadeus* and *Bridgerton*, with elements of the swashbuckling heroism of *The Three Musketeers* and, occasionally, the absurdity of *Blackadder*.

Born in Guadeloupe to a Black enslaved mother and a plantation-owning French father, Saint-Georges (as he preferred to be known) moved in the highest echelons of French society, negotiating its petty squabbles, hypocritical morals and gossipy obsession with status. As a 'gendarme de la garde du roi' (hence 'chevalier') he had direct contact with Louis XV and, later, Louis XVI and Marie Antoinette at Versailles, while also being immersed in the world of *liaisons dangereuses* at the Palais-Royal, seedbed of the Revolution. A leader of the French abolitionist movement, Saint-Georges commanded the first Black regiment in Europe, yet also spent time in prison when the Revolution started to devour its young. Amid all this, he was among the foremost violinists and composers in France, as well as conductor of the largest, most renowned orchestra in Europe.

As with his fencing displays, his violin concertos offered Parisians the chance to witness the advanced skills of Saint-Georges. This G major concerto's first movement leaps nimbly across the violin's registers and the soloist often soars above the orchestra (rising an octave higher than anything found in Mozart's concertos), before plunging to its lowest notes. This all comes within a *style galant* work of polite restraint, a mirror to the social conventions of *Ancien Régime* France. It was probably first performed by Saint-Georges while he also directed his own orchestra, the Concert des Amateurs, which combined musicians from official orchestras with talented members of the *bourgoisie*. These were 'amateurs' in the literal sense: lovers of music, friends relishing their congenial music-making, resulting in a palpable *joie de vivre* that is simply irresistible. ●

Christopher Dingle is Professor of Music and Director of the French Music Research Hub at the Royal Birmingham Conservatoire. He is the editor of Schott Music's Saint-Georges Edition and is currently preparing a book on the composer. He is also author or editor of books on Messiaen, Julian Anderson and music criticism.

Joseph Bologne, Chevalier de Saint-Georges Violin Concerto in G major, Op. 8
23 JULY

The Future of Music

ROYAL

COLLEGE

OF MUSIC

London

Experience an inspiring
education at the
Royal College of Music

Apply now for 2026 entry
rcm.ac.uk/study

Global No. 1 for Music & Performing Arts
QS World University Rankings 2025/2024/2023/2022

Viennese Whirl

This season the Proms celebrates 200 years since the birth of Johann Strauss II, the star of 19th-century Vienna's dance-music heyday. Ahead of a special Viennese concert, **RICHARD BRATBY** unwraps the history of an irresistible musical tradition which, despite its reputation for frivolity, had a major impact on 'serious' composers

There's a story that's told in Vienna of how, in the Great Plague year of 1679, a balladeer named Marx Augustin decided to drown his worries in wine. He succeeded a little too well: staggering home, he tripped, unconscious, into a plague pit. A few hours later he awoke with a throbbing head, and used his bagpipes to summon rescuers. 'Oh, my dear Augustin / All is lost!', he sang to a melody that a century and a quarter later might have been described as a waltz. Capturing the spirit of the city in song, 'Ei, du lieber Augustin' became – in the words of the Viennese historian Hilde Spiel – 'the first true *Wienerlied*'.

And if – like any good myth – this tale has only a very sketchy relationship with fact, at least part of it has the ring of truth. In Vienna's final century as an imperial capital its citizens perfected a fine art of surviving dark times with light music. Not a single generation avoided political or military trauma – wars, revolutions, stock market crashes. But when history gave the Viennese lemons, they grated the zest and sprinkled it over dance music of unprecedented sophistication and beauty. If we still imagine those tumultuous years as a golden age of civilised pleasure, it's largely due to the music that filled Vienna's many cafés, ballrooms and *Heurigen* (suburban wine gardens).

◀ Emperor Franz Joseph I of Austria waltzes at a ball held at Vienna's Hofburg palace; painting by Wilhelm Gause (1853–1916)

That pleasure took many forms. Popular songs (such as Gustav Pick's wildly popular 'Fiakerlied' – literally 'The Cabbie's Song') were an old tradition, and small-scale wine-garden bands (violins, clarinet and a guitar or zither) were widespread long before the Schrammel brothers formed their famous trio in the late 1870s – giving their name to an entire genre of genial, folk-flavoured song and dance, 'Schrammelmusik'. But to the wider world the music of Vienna meant the seductive lilt of the waltz. Schubert and Hummel had waltzed in moderation but in the 1820s, in the hands of Johann Strauss I and his friend (and later rival) Joseph Lanner, this sensuous, subversive dance escaped the suburbs to intoxicate first the city and then the world. Strauss himself attracted rock-star levels of adulation. 'His hair is curly, his mouth is melodious, energetic,' gasped one admirer in 1833. Berlioz, Schumann and Queen Victoria were all devoted fans.

Strauss lived fast and died young, leaving his orchestra – and his nickname of 'Waltz King' – to his estranged son Johann II. Along with his brothers Eduard and the former civil engineer Josef (whom he always insisted was 'the most talented of us all'), Johann II would become the most beloved of all Viennese composers, conquering Europe, Russia and even America. Nor was he merely a popular success. Johann Strauss II might have been the only musician whom both Richard Wagner (who authorised Strauss's orchestra to premiere excerpts from

Tristan and Isolde in Vienna) and Johannes Brahms addressed as 'Meister'.

Brahms and Wagner each sensed something profound in this outwardly playful music. True, the Strausses were commercial artists, and they often worked to a formula. But (like the authentic recipe for *Sachertorte*) creating a truly irresistible formula takes something like genius. Vienna's empire supplied the ingredients: German *Ländler*, Czech polkas, Polish mazurkas, the songs of synagogue cantors and the melodies of Roma gypsies. The ceremonial *élan* of the Habsburg armies gave a special zip to Viennese marches and galops; and fashions from Paris – the quadrille and Offenbach's comic operettas – were embraced with passion. The paprika tingle of Hungarian folk music is never far away.

But nor is a long-breathed *bel canto* lyricism (Austria lost its last Italian-speaking territories only in 1919). The earliest waltzes moved in tight, four-square phrases. The Strausses liberated their melodies to sing over the bar-lines – expressive, caressing and charged with that most potent (but elusive) of qualities: nostalgia. The ravishingly scored introductions and codas to waltzes such as *By the Beautiful Blue Danube* or Josef Strauss's *Harmony of the Spheres* transform dance music into something not far from a symphonic poem. 'Each waltz is a little love story of bashful courtship, impulsive infatuation, radiant happiness,' wrote the critic Eduard Hanslick, adding, 'and here and there a little breath of melancholy.'

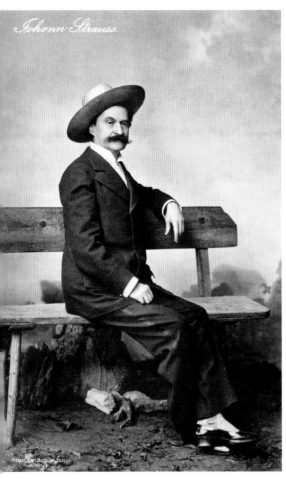

'Waltz King' Johann Strauss II depicted on a 19th-century postcard; an international celebrity, Strauss came to define the sound of Viennese dance music, earning the respect of more 'serious' composers such as Wagner and Brahms along the way

Those flavours saturated the music of a new generation of Austro-Hungarian popular composers – operetta masters such as Franz Lehár, Oscar Straus (no relation), Emmerich Kálmán and Robert Stolz, who created happiness under the darkening skies of the 20th century. Countless 'serious' composers embraced Strauss's bittersweet beauty – Brahms in his *Liebeslieder Waltzes*, Ravel in *La valse* and Richard Strauss (also no relation, much to his regret) in his operas *Der Rosenkavalier* and *Arabella*. Schoenberg and his progressive disciples crafted jewel-like arrangements of Strauss waltzes, while Mahler distilled their yearning, and their whirling momentum, into the scherzos of his symphonies.

And, after the fall of the Habsburgs, Vienna's exiles took their music with them. Viennese operetta, as much as jazz, shaped the Broadway of Jerome Kern and the Gershwins (George and Ira's song 'By Strauss' might be the sincerest tribute ever paid by America to old Europe), and waltzes sweep through the scores of *Show Boat* (1927), *Carousel* (1945), *My Fair Lady* (1956) and *A Little Night Music* (1973). In Hollywood, meanwhile, Viennese composers such as Max Steiner (whose grandfather had commissioned Strauss's *Die Fledermaus*) and Erich Korngold defined the sound of cinema. Korngold's final orchestral work, *Straussiana* (1953), takes melodies by Johann Strauss II and dresses them in shimmering orchestration – a bouquet on the grave of a vanished world, dedicated to the school orchestras of America.

But there was hope as well as sorrow in Korngold's gesture, and 200 years after the birth of Johann Strauss II it would be premature to assume that the story is at an end. There's a reason why Stanley Kubrick, in *2001: A Space Odyssey*, chose *The Blue Danube* to symbolise human civilisation at its peak. Western culture is so deeply saturated with the Viennese light music legacy that perhaps we no longer even notice it. Johann Strauss II left his wife Adele an ebony baton that he had inherited from the operetta composer Franz von Suppé. She presented it to Franz Lehár, who in turn passed it to Robert Stolz – who called it 'the sceptre of the Waltz Kings', though he did not use it when, aged 79, he conducted his own song, 'Du hast mich so fascziniert', as Austria's entry in the 1960 Eurovision Song Contest.

Stolz began his musical life playing for Brahms and ended it on TV sets across Europe. He thought of himself as the last in a line, and it's true that from the Great Plague to the glitter of Eurovision is a very long dance indeed. But wherever classical music transcends social boundaries – and whenever popular music becomes great art – the spirit of Vienna takes the floor. This is still Johann Strauss II's world. We're just dancing in it. ●

Richard Bratby is Chief Classical Music Critic of *The Spectator* and writes on music and culture for *Gramophone*, *Bachtrack* and *The Critic*. His latest book, *Refiner's Fire: The Academy of Ancient Music and the Historical Performance Revolution*, was published in 2023.

Viennese Whirl
2 AUGUST

Arvo in Parts

When the music of Estonian composer Arvo Pärt first came to the West during the 1980s, listeners were immediately drawn to its deeply moving, spiritual quality. Rejecting the modernist style of his earlier work of the 1960s, Pärt underwent a radical self-appraisal. Inspired by Gregorian chant and Renaissance polyphony, and by his conversion to the Orthodox Church, he created a daringly stripped-back approach whose appeal was practically universal – one that has nourished his subsequent works for 45 years. As the Proms celebrates the composer's 90th birthday, **MAARJA TYLER**, a Researcher at the Arvo Pärt Centre in Estonia, draws on archival material and personal interviews to present a series of scenes in the life of a composer whose music continues to speak directly to the human soul

For works by Arvo Pärt at the Proms,
see Index of Works, pages 165–167

All ears: Arvo Pärt in Berlin, 2007

1951

We are in Rakvere, a small town in the east of Soviet-occupied Estonia. Arvo Pärt's classes at the local high school have just finished, and, taking leave of his friends, the 16-year-old heads over to the local kindergarten, where his mother is a teacher. He frequently visits her here, and improvises on the piano to accompany the stories that are the basis of the children's theatrical games.

The young Pärt does not realise the musical journey that lies ahead of him (this is 60 years before the music website *Bachtrack* cites him as the world's most-performed living composer), but it's here – surrounded by the imaginations of children – that he begins to learn the beauty of music's communicative and emotional power. The seeds of his heightened musical sensitivity are sown.

1964

Pärt has graduated from the Tallinn Conservatory and is now a member of the Union of Soviet Composers. Despite fast becoming a leading figure in the Soviet avant-garde, he begins to feel hesistant towards modernism – a shift first seen in *Collage über B-A-C-H* (1964), one of a number of works in which he uses a collage technique to create contrasts. In this piece the contrast is between the dissonant sound he has until now been exploring and the harmonious music of J. S. Bach. This return to an earlier point in musical history marks a rift between Pärt's modernist aesthetics and his growing quest for beauty, purity and perfection, a shift that will deepen in the coming years.

1968

His 12-tone, or 'serial', compositions (placing the notes in a predetermined order) are sparking interest in Estonia and abroad, and the 33-year-old Pärt appears to be at the peak of his career. Yet it is at this moment, with *Credo* (1968) – the most dramatic example of his collage works – that Pärt's modernist chapter abruptly closes.

Credo sees a return to Bach: the solo piano part is based on the Prelude in C major from *The Well-Tempered Clavier*. But Pärt for the first time also introduces direct religious references, with the choir performing fragments from the Christian Creed ('I believe in Jesus Christ …') and Jesus's Sermon on the Mount. With this turning point in his spiritual and musical journeys, he feels that his reliance on collage has reached its limit.

Pärt at his home in 1969; the time at which he descended into an eight-year crisis over his musical direction

'Bettering the world does not begin from the opposite end of the world, but from within yourself … This needs to be a school of shaping the soul, not merely a school of composition': words by Arvo Pärt at one of the Arvo Pärt Centre's permanent exhibitions

1976

For over seven years, Pärt has withdrawn from public life, focusing on the spiritual tradition of the Eastern Orthodox Church and immersing himself in medieval and Renaissance music. Delving deeper into the fundamentals of music, he limits himself to writing single-line melodies. His musical diaries fill with them – without time signatures, bar-lines, rhythm, key or dynamics. He describes this reduction as a way to restore his sensitivity to sound. Gaining confidence, he explores adding a second voice. Pärt experiments until he discovers the simple beauty of triads (the three harmonious notes that form the basis of a simple chord). Meticulously, he searches for the best way to incorporate them. The result is *Für Alina* (1976), a piano miniature with a gentle melody accompanied by triads, organised according to his own set of rules. Pärt's famous compositional technique – 'tintinnabuli' – is born.

1979

Since composing *Für Alina*, Pärt has refined his musical language, creating more than 10 compositions in three years. From this creative surge (1976–8), his best-known works have emerged: *Summa*, *Cantus in memoriam Benjamin Britten*, *Tabula rasa*, *Fratres* and *Spiegel im Spiegel*. While composing *Missa syllabica* (1977), Pärt discovers a method combining tintinnabuli with a technique where music is derived from text. This opens new creative possibilities, allowing him to write music for sacred texts. However, his increasing religiosity, his distancing from the Communist regime and his growing reputation in the West make life in Soviet Estonia untenable. Facing pressure from the authorities, Pärt and his family have no choice but to leave his country. Permission is granted due to his wife Nora's Jewish heritage. They pack seven bags and board a train with no fixed destination.

1985

By now, Pärt and his family have made a new life in West Berlin. Following the 1984 release of the album *Tabula rasa*, featuring Gidon Kremer, Keith Jarrett and others, he gains a growing number of admirers. At this moment, another creative turning point takes place. He receives a letter from British choral conductor Paul Hillier expressing plans to perform Pärt's vocal pieces with the Hilliard Ensemble in London. Invited to rehearsals, Pärt and Nora arrive at St Mary's Church in Woodford on a warm June day. They hear no singing upon entering the church, since Hillier has paused to discuss a point of phrasing. As *Summa* resumes, Pärt's tintinnabuli music shimmers through the space, bright yet warm thanks to the singers' flawless intonation. Pärt is overwhelmed – it's as if he is meeting his music for the first time.

St Silouan of Mount Athos (1866–1938), a monk of the Eastern Orthodox Church, to which Pärt converted in 1972

Composing in his studio in Berlin, 1990

1990

During the final years of the Soviet Union, the ban on Pärt's music (imposed due to his exile) was gradually lifted, allowing his works to return to Estonian concert halls. It was then that Estonian conductor Tõnu Kaljuste's bold and distinctive interpretation of *Te Deum* (1985) left a lasting impression on Pärt, marking the beginning of an enduring musical friendship and the revival of his connection with Estonia. Pärt's long-awaited visits to his homeland also rekindled ties with Estonian musicians, who would go on to become invaluable performers of his music around the world. By this time, Arvo Pärt has become an established composer, receiving commissions worldwide and composing music in the tintinnabuli style he developed in 1976.

2010

Arvo Pärt finishes one of his most significant works, *Adam's Lament*, for string orchestra and mixed choir. He has carried its idea in his mind since the late 1980s. The piece is inspired by the Russian prose text of the same title by St Silouan of Mount Athos, reflecting on the life and regrets of humanity's biblical forefather, Adam. This composition encapsulates the two crucial streams of Pärt's creative foundation: the history of Western music and the spiritual heritage of the Eastern Orthodox tradition. Compared to earlier vocal works, such as *Stabat mater* (1985), *Miserere* (1989), *Litany* (1994) and *Kanon Pokajanen* (1997), in *Adam's Lament* Pärt employs tintinnabuli more freely, a characteristic that will define his compositions in the following decade.

2024

Arvo Pärt now lives in the quiet of the forest near Laulasmaa beach in Estonia – a long stretch of pale sand facing the Gulf of Finland. In 2018, the Arvo Pärt Centre opened in Laulasmaa as a home for his archive, spanning hundreds of works, from small-scale pieces to major commissions from figures and institutions as varied as the Princess of Monaco and the Tate Gallery. One November afternoon, I guide a group of excited children through the Centre's gently curved interior. Arvo, now 89 and retired but often at the Centre, greets us. Little is said – his smiling eyes communicate all – but I sense he would love to improvise for them at the piano, as he once used to. Times have changed, however, and his fleeting improvisations have blossomed into a remarkable body of unique compositions, in which every sound is worthy of love.

The Arvo Pärt Centre in the coastal location of Laulasmaa, Estonia; opened in 2018, it houses the composer's archive, performance and exhibition spaces and a café; its tower features a viewing platform

With conductor Tõnu Kaljuste, who has collaborated with Pärt for over 30 years

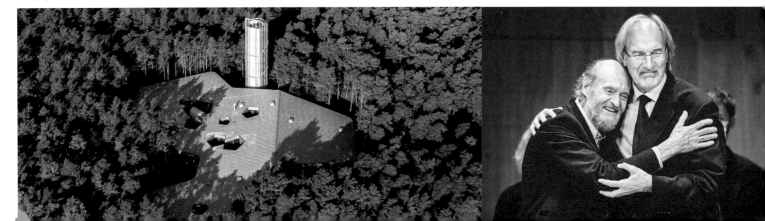

Find your future at Alleyn's

Co-educational excellence for children aged 11-18

We offer scholarships and bursaries

#AllWeCanBe

ALLEYN'S
1619

alleyns.org.uk

BRISTOL BEACON

SOUNDS BETTER WITH YOU

Never miss a moment at bristolbeacon.org

Supported using public funding by
ARTS COUNCIL
ENGLAND

ROYAL PHILHARMONIC ORCHESTRA

2025–26 SEASON

Royal Philharmonic Orchestra Live at Cadogan Hall

Acclaimed international artists including

Kevin John Edusei (*Conductor-in-Residence, 2025–26*),
Boris Giltburg, Pavel Kolesnikov, Midori, Makoto Ozone,
Masabane Cecilia Rangwanasha, Alexander Shelley,
Nicky Spence OBE, Sir John Rutter and Nil Venditti

Captivating composers

Beethoven, Copland, Dvořák, Elgar,
Gershwin, Joe Hisaishi, Mendelssohn,
Dora Pejačević, Rachmaninov, Ravel,
Sibelius, Stravinsky and more

Orchestral music lives here

Book now at rpo.co.uk/cadoganhall

CADOGAN HALL

SOUTHBANK CENTRE

This is classical music in the 21st century

AUTUMN/WINTER 2025/26

BOOK NOW

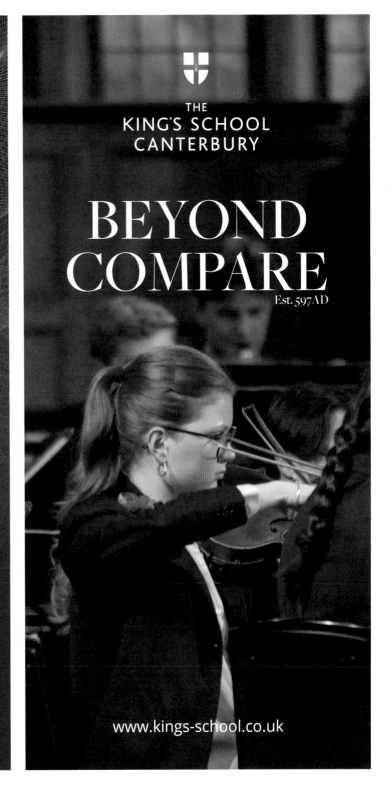

THE KING'S SCHOOL CANTERBURY

BEYOND COMPARE
Est. 597AD

www.kings-school.co.uk

NICHOLAS SPICE
explores the ways in which music has been reflected in literary fiction over the past two centuries, and asks whether its essence can really be distilled into words

Faust and Mephistopheles by Eugène Delacroix (1798–1863); Thomas Mann's novel *Doctor Faustus* reimagines the Faust legend, recasting its antihero as the fictitious composer Adrian Leverkühn

Words and Music

The ethical crux of Ian McEwan's *Amsterdam* – the scene around which the novel crystallises – is structured as a test of character for the protagonist, a test which he ignominiously fails. Clive Linley is a distinguished composer at the peak of his career. He has been commissioned to write a symphony for the official concert celebrating the millennium. It is to be the crowning glory of his work, setting the seal upon his reputation as the leading composer of the nation. The deadline approaches. Inspiration is failing him. He needs a melody for the final movement, which will gather to itself the expressive significance of the entire work. He travels to the Lake District to walk in the hills alone. At the very moment when the muse speaks, he catches sight of a disturbing scene below him: a woman is being violently assaulted by a man. Knowing that, if he goes to her aid, the elusive melody will slip from his grasp, he ducks down and heads off in the opposite direction. Later, he will learn that the woman was raped and that the man was the 'Lake District rapist', long sought by the police.

Linley's failure to act is not represented in *Amsterdam* as the tragic lapse of an essentially decent man, and his dilemma does not engage our sympathies (unlike, say, Razumov's in Joseph Conrad's *Under Western Eyes*). Linley is a hollow man and his sin of omission confirms him as a moral bankrupt. The scene is chilling, and McEwan handles it with his customary brilliance, but Linley's ethical quandary isn't especially subtle: it's obvious what he should do and unsurprising that he doesn't do it. Another novelist might have weighted the two sides of the dilemma more evenly – Iris Murdoch for example, for whom the relation between aesthetic and ethical value was of absorbing interest.

In her short philosophical work *The Sovereignty of Good*, Murdoch explored the question 'Can the Beautiful be a Form of the Good?'. Answering this in the affirmative, she cited works of literature (by Thucydides) and the visual arts (by Titian), but she left music to one side, partly because, like many intellectuals, she knew little about it, but more importantly because music and morality share no obvious common ground. Music may be well or badly written but it cannot be said to have any ethical qualities – it makes no sense, as it were, to speak of an intrinsically evil piece of music. No piece of music could frame a moral dilemma of the kind depicted in McEwan's novel – it is not Linley's melody that is evil but his behaviour.

What one might call music's radical irresponsibility – its only kind of truth being to itself – is beautifully captured in W. H. Auden's poem 'Anthem for St Cecilia's Day', set to music for *a cappella*

Helena Bonham Carter as Helen Schlegel in James Ivory's 1992 film adaptation of *Howards End*; Schlegel, in E. M. Forster's original novel, imagines in the third movement of Beethoven's Fifth Symphony 'a goblin walking quietly over the universe, from end to end'

choir by Benjamin Britten. There, music is personified as an eternal child:

> *I cannot grow;*
> *I have no shadow*
> *To run away from,*
> *I only play.*
>
> *I cannot err;*
> *There is no creature*
> *Whom I belong to,*
> *Whom I could wrong.*

Notwithstanding music's intrinsic moral neutrality, its effect on us has at various times in history been thought to be depraving. Because of its origins in dance and its appeal to the senses, music has usually been disapproved of by puritans of every stripe. To the theologically unbending, the power of music to move us, to stir us to states of excitement and elation, even ecstasy, has confirmed their suspicions that it might consort

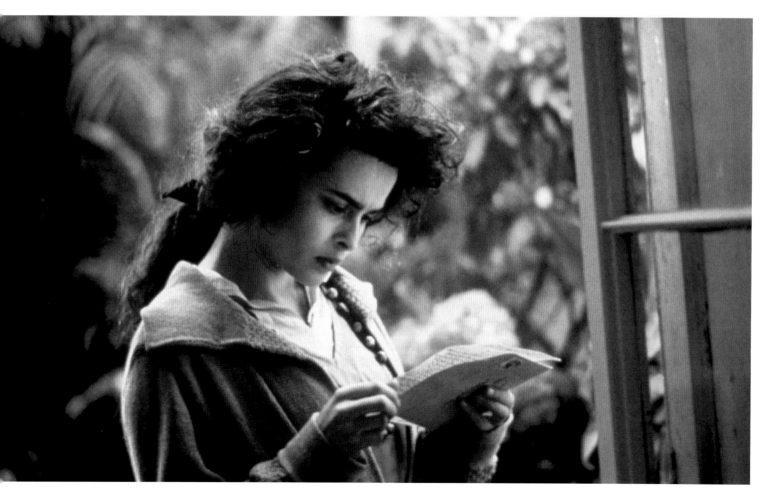

with dark forces, even the Devil himself. In the Middle Ages, the tritone (an augmented fourth, or diminished fifth) was called the Devil's interval. In the 18th century, the violinist Giuseppe Tartini reported that the Devil had appeared to him in a dream and dictated a sonata of incomparable brilliance, a pale copy of which he wrote down on awakening – the so-called 'Devil's Trill' Sonata.

In literature, the association of music with occult powers is central to the greatest novel about music ever written: Thomas Mann's *Doctor Faustus*. Whether the protagonist of the story – the composer Adrian Leverkühn – actually meets the Devil or merely hallucinates the encounter is left ambiguous, but literal actuality has little relevance to the incident: psychically, the event takes place and seems to fit naturally with Leverkühn's sense of himself as a being apart. Mann, or rather, Mann's narrator – in his own way, an unreliable source – depicts Adrian as, from childhood, introverted and aloof, disdainful of the world and only truly at home in the alternative reality inside his head. The processes of musical creation are represented in the novel as remote from ordinary human thought processes – as indeed involving abstruse imaginings framed in an esoteric language. Leverkühn slips at will from everyday speech into his own, strange, cod-medieval German, evocative of magical practices, alchemy – necromancy even.

Doctor Faustus sits at the pinnacle of a tradition that originated in the writings of German novelists and philosophers at the turn of the 19th century. The lectures of Wendell Kretschmar, Adrian's composition teacher and mentor, suggest an unbroken line back to E. T. A. Hoffmann's *Kreisleriana*. For Kretschmar, as for Hoffmann, it is in the works of Beethoven that music fulfils its true destiny – Beethoven, that 'lonely prince of a realm of spirits, from whom now only a chilling breath issued to terrify his most willing contemporaries, standing as they did aghast at these communications of which only at moments, only by exception, they could understand anything at all.'

The notion that music spoke in a higher language – in Hoffmann's words, 'the language of that unknown, romantic spirit-realm' – amounted to a startling recalibration of the scale of artistic value. Immanual Kant had expressed a conventional view of the matter when, in the *Critique of Judgement*, he wrote of music as coming last in the hierarchy of the arts, after the 'arts of speech' and the 'figurative arts', on the grounds that 'it merely plays with sensations'. Music's inability to represent things had prompted a similar downgrading from the encyclopedist Jean d'Alembert. By contrast, for Romantic thinkers, it was precisely in its freedom from the constraints of linguistic or figurative representation that music was superior.

If music speaks of things beyond language, then it follows that the essence of music itself cannot be grasped by words. The musician and critic Hans Keller thought that only music could comment on music; while the French literary philosopher Roland Barthes deplored the inescapability of the adjective in literary accounts of it ('parlour game: discuss a piece of music without using a single adjective'). In this respect, it's interesting and not a little paradoxical that, just at the moment when philosophers were rethinking music as a form of knowledge beyond words, composers – notably Beethoven – began to supplement the standard tempo indications (Allegro, Andante, *etc.*) with adjectives describing how they wanted their music played.

The promotion of music to top art form roughly coincided with the rise of the novel and the evolution of a narrative discourse capable of the subtlest representations of social reality. As such, the purposes of the novel and the purposes of music could hardly be further from one another, and, not surprisingly, novelists have tended to steer clear of music as a subject for their books. Composers and performers crop up as characters in novels from time to time, but there are very few major novels in which descriptions of music figure to any significant extent and when they do it's hard not to sympathise with Roland Barthes. One thinks, for example, of the celebrated passage in E. M. Forster's *Howards End*, where Helen Schlegel, inspired to heights of poetical fantasy by Beethoven's Fifth Symphony, sees in the first theme of the Scherzo 'a goblin walking quietly over the universe, from

Johannes Kreisler – E. T. A. Hoffmann's composer protagonist (and alter ego) from his trilogy *Kreisleriana* – pictured here 'with respectable citizens' in a drawing by Rainer Ehrt (born 1960), itself based on Hoffmann's original illustration

end to end'. The triumphant affirmation of the finale chases the goblin away, only for the momentary reappearance of the Scherzo theme near the end of the movement to darken the picture once more: 'The goblins were there. They could return.' Helen's imaginings show a clear kinship with E. T. A. Hoffmann's effusions in his 1820 essay on the same symphony, and it is evidently Forster's intention that we should read the passage more as casting light on Helen than on Beethoven.

Whatever it is that music means for us, it accompanies us through our daily lives, occupying imaginative space and flowing in and out of our thoughts, feelings and memories. Marcel Proust's supreme representation of the phenomenology of human experience, *À la recherche du temps perdu* ('In Search of Lost Time'), finds a special place for music within the economy of the mind. For Monsieur Swann, a particular passage in a violin and piano sonata by the (fictional) composer Vinteuil, has an effect upon him analogous to that of the exquisite scent of a rose or the face of a woman fleetingly glimpsed in the street – experiences, all of them, of an indefinable quality, opening new spaces in the soul: 'But then at a certain moment, without being able to distinguish any clear outline, or to give a name to what was pleasing him, suddenly enraptured, he had tried to grasp the phrase or harmony – he did not know which – that had just been played and that had opened and expanded his soul, as the fragrance of

certain roses, wafted upon the moist air of the evening, has the power of dilating one's nostrils.'

In the history of aesthetics, few propositions have been cited as often as Walter Pater's that 'All art constantly aspires to the condition of music', one interpretation of which might be that what, ultimately, we value in great art of any kind is its ineffability – its power to silence us. Another way to put this would be to say that we value the things in art that cannot be paraphrased, cannot be reduced to adjectives. We prize such moments in painting, poetry, architecture and dance, as much as in music. In the novel – a sprawling portmanteau form – they may strike us in individual sentences or paragraphs, or in the depiction of a character, or the drama of a scene of narrative crisis.

But, above all, it is in the imagining of worlds akin to, but different from, our world, that the novel, at its greatest, achieves the ineffable, the unutterable, the thing that leaves us speechless: the world of Proust's Combray, or of Italy in James's *Portrait of a Lady* or Hardy's Blackmoor Vale in *Tess of the d'Urbervilles*. Of these, we can no more say what gives them their unique reality than we can describe the taste of a madeleine, the scent of a rose, the beauty of a face seen in a moment of unselfconscious expression – or the turn of an inspired musical phrase. ●

Nicholas Spice is Consulting Publisher at the *London Review of Books*, of which he was Publisher from 1982 until 2021, and to which he has regularly contributed articles on literature and music.

ONE FOR MY BABY

From lullabies to baby classes and concerts, there are many ways to introduce very young children to music. Early childhood music researcher **JESSICA PITT** explores the important role music plays in an infant's development, as well as the positive impact it can have later in life

was listening to BBC Radio 4's *Today* in that restful week between Christmas and New Year, when guest editors are asked to shape programming based on their own areas of interest. One of those guests, Baroness Floella Benjamin, included discussion of a subject close to her heart: that of children, childhood and the arts. 'Childhood,' she said, 'lasts a lifetime', and there is research from the disciplines of neuroscience, psychology and sociology that supports this. Our earliest experiences – perhaps especially those that occur before we have acquired language – are the hardest wired, directly shaping our adult lives. And music, if allowed, can play an enormously beneficial role in this.

Early encounters with the arts bring children into dialogue with the material world. When their senses and intellect are engaged, children can express their unique identity: seeing, hearing, moving, vocalising and touching can help them to know themselves as distinct from others. Early creative learning environments allow for curiosity, imagination and social and communicative skills to flourish. They are also a safe space in which to fail – an important step in building positive dispositions for perseverance and critical thinking. Such foundational experiences provide the building blocks for what Aristotle called *eudaimonia*, or living a flourishing life.

Kid rock: the earliest encounters with music and music-making are thought to be beneficial for very young children

That music specifically should be so important should not come as a surprise. It is, after all, central to the most important relationship for our survival as infants, namely that between parent and child. If you have ever watched a parent in close 'conversation' with their baby you may have noticed how the adult's face becomes animated with a broad smile. Their eyes widen, and they speak with a sing-song quality, repeating lyrics rhythmically. Given the chance, the baby is likely to respond with similar vocal patterns, with attempts to copy the mouth shapes of the adult. The word content of the interchange has no meaning to the baby: it is the emotional narrative that matters. Biologists and musicologists have named this interaction Communicative Musicality, and it is thought to contribute to our motivation to make and create music.

Music continues to thread through the early years. From being sung lullabies (which has, incidentally, been found to calm the singing adult too) to being bounced on the lap to 'The Wheels on the Bus', or by listening to music on long journeys, young children acquire a rich repertoire. Pulse, rhythm, melody, harmony, tempo and dynamics – even structure – are all absorbed. Not named, or consciously recognised, but the stuff of music is felt and remembered. You may have noticed very young children humming or vocalising as they play alone. This helps regulate emotions and aids concentration. Children as young as 2 have been found to take snippets of known songs and rework them by combining phrases from different melodies and adding their own original lyrics to create 'potpourri' songs. This ability to be creative, and to improvise during play, reveals a sophisticated musical competence. In these moments children appear to be in a world of their own – in a state of flow where time stands still and concentration is at its peak, a state found by psychologists to be optimal for learning.

66 Pulse, rhythm, melody, harmony, tempo, dynamics – even structure – are all absorbed. Not named, or consciously recognised, but the stuff of music is felt and remembered. 99

We are lucky here in the UK. Musical activities for the very young are available in a variety of settings, from hospitals to libraries to theatres to concert halls, as well as in the classroom. Much of the justification for these initiatives comes from neuroscience and psychology research. Studies have found that early engagement with active music training can affect the brain's structure and functioning. Music training fine-tunes the auditory system, which can help children identify and process speech sounds (phonological awareness). This in turn benefits the skills needed for reading and writing. Active music training can also boost verbal learning and memory –

Psychological studies also demonstrate the social and emotional benefits of music. Joint music-making – drumming together, for example – has been found to influence pro-social behaviour and feelings of cohesion in groups of children as young as 4. Music is a temporal art form that co-ordinates experiences in time: it enables bodies to synchronise (heartbeats have been found to align in group music sessions). Tension and release – inherent properties of music – also create a communal emotional experience. These seemingly magical properties have been harnessed across all cultures and across many thousands of years for ritual and celebration, acting to build belonging and community. No wonder, then, that parents too have been found to benefit from attending early years music groups.

Concerts for very young children offer another entry point for musical enrichment. They provide an excellent introduction to the music of our own culture as well as that of others – and for children to experience others *doing* art, stimulating a desire for them do this themselves.

If parents want their children to embark on formal music training, Western classical music offers several models that have been developed since the early 20th century. One of the best known for instrumental learning is the Suzuki method, developed by Japanese violinist Shinichi Suzuki (1898–1998). It requires an active role from parents, and prioritises listening and playing by ear before reading music. Like Suzuki,

String when you're winning: Suzuki's method for learning a musical instrument requires an active role from parents, who are encouraged to learn it alongside their child

very useful in the early childhood years, when a huge amount of knowledge must be assimilated. Precisely *which* aspect of music training causes these changes in the brain is more difficult to pinpoint, and we are advised by researchers to be cautious in stating that music makes us 'smarter'.

Hungarian composer and educator Zoltán Kodály (1882–1967) believed that every young child has musical aptitude and should have the best possible musical experiences. He went so far as to argue that music provides an intellectual nourishment that nothing else can. His own approach starts with the voice, based on the folk-song and -dance repertoire of a child's country of birth, in the belief that singing is foundational to the development of 'inner hearing' – valuable for subsequent instrumental learning.

Swiss composer and educator Émile Jaques-Dalcroze (1865–1950) built on this idea, identifying the need to develop an inner sense of pulse and rhythm. His Eurhythmics exercises help learners to move musically. One example requires a child to adjust their movements in space and time as they walk to music, with the aim of arriving at a certain spot by the end of the phrase. For German composer and educator Carl Orff (1895–1982), very young children learn best through play. His own approach was based on a holisitic view of music learning that combined movement, music, speech and drama in playful activities. All four of these approaches are prevalent in music education offered for young children in the UK today.

Interestingly, there is no evidence that formal musical training in early childhood is essential to achieving at the highest musical levels later in life. (Though indicators show that a supportive home environment – one that encourages spontaneous expression – does boost

chances.) But the unequivocal benefits of music-making, for both children and their accompanying adults, are not necessarily concerned with training professionals: they help to build well-rounded, social, emotionally sensitive human beings.

All young children have potential, and all are motivated and excited by their own playful engagement with music. To be around this is infectious. In a recent Arts Council England study I helped to facilitate, an early childhood artist told us that 'working with babies has been the most extraordinary experience for me and my practice – literally a game-changer'. Another discovered how 'young children have incredible capacities for connection and creativity, and my role is to open the door for that … taking their imaginative and creative input seriously'.

If, as Floella Benjamin says, childhood lasts a lifetime, what sorts of experiences would best support a child on their lifetime journey with music? Answering this question requires adults to spend time with young children, to play with them – to enter a world that isn't dependent on words, and to do so without focusing on outcomes. This is when music truly speaks. And by reacquainting ourselves with our inner child we allow for fresh responses to music in our own lives too. Because, in Kodály's words, 'in every great artist the child is alive'. ●

Jessica Pitt sits on the Early Childhood Music Education Commission of the International Society of Music Education and on the board of directors for Sound Sense. She is an Academic Programmes professor at the Royal College of Music and co-directs the early years arts organisation Magic Acorns.

Proms to enjoy with your family

The BBC Proms is a great place to introduce your family to classical music, with half-price tickets available for under-18s at every concert. The following Proms offer younger listeners a brilliant first-time experience. Programmes feature film-music staples and iconic classical favourites, and there are two CBeebies concerts designed specifically for children.

CBeebies Prom: Wildlife Jamboree
Royal Northern Sinfonia
GATESHEAD • 27 JULY, 1.30pm & 4pm

Viennese Whirl
BBC Concert Orchestra/Anna-Maria Helsing
2 AUGUST

Relaxed Prom: The Planets
National Youth Orchestra/Tess Jackson
10 AUGUST

Shostakovich's Fifth by Heart
Aurora Orchestra/Nicholas Collon
16 & 17 AUGUST

CBeebies Prom: A Magical Bedtime Story
Sinfonia Smith Square/Ellie Slorach
25 AUGUST, 12.30pm & 3.30pm

African Symphony
Angélique Kidjo, BBC Philharmonic Orchestra/ Chris Cameron
BRADFORD • 7 SEPTEMBER

Discover ...

FREDERICK DELIUS'S
A Mass of Life

JEREMY DIBBLE celebrates an ambitious English choral work that takes the Mass out of the church and places it among the people

Completed in 1905, Delius's *A Mass of Life* stands as a truly grand project – by far his largest symphonic canvas. With its unique synthesis of opera, orchestral tone-poem and ballet music, it drove the composer to new heights of inspiration. The work is as profoundly life-affirming as it is demanding of its singers and players. What was Delius aiming at? This inimitable iconoclast and unapologetic atheist by no means identified with the English choral tradition of his contemporaries Sullivan, Parry, Stanford and Elgar and its links to Christianity. Instead, he sought to celebrate the philosopher Friedrich Nietzsche's idea of the 'Übermensch' (Superman) posited in *Also sprach Zarathustra* by creating a new, vibrant secular Mass.

The die is cast in the imposing opening chorus, 'O thou my will' (and what an opening it is), which asserts the resolve and unquenchable spirit of the prophet Zarathustra, the work's central character. His energy and zest for life have a commanding presence in the dance movements, especially in the infectious yet unconventional chorus 'Now for a dance' and as the young girls dance in the meadow. Caught up in the headiness of Nieztsche's obsession with Dionysus (the Greek god of wine and festivities), Delius called these 'Dance Songs'. Zarathustra's 'journey' (which, perhaps ironically, has many parallels with the story of Jesus in the Christian Gospels) also has its moments of sadness and solitary

meditation. We hear this in the baritone solo 'Woe is me! Whither is time fled?'. We hear it too in the inward contemplation of the following choral nocturne for Zarathustra ('Night reigneth'), one of the composer's most passionate, quasi-operatic creations (the climax is one of Delius's most compelling); and in the second nocturne, for baritone ('God's woe is deeper'). But what dominates the *Mass* are the evocative nature music of Part 2, so typical of Delius's beloved pastoral landscapes, and the sense of boundless joy in the face of death, symbolised by the majestic end of the final movement ('O man, mark well!) in rapt music that seems to recall Wagner's opera *Tristan and Isolde. A Mass of Life* proved, significantly, to be a pivotal moment of self-discovery and propelled Delius forward into an early 20th-century, modernist, Austro-German arena shared with Strauss, Schoenberg, Reger, Mahler, Zemlinsky and Pfitzner.

Delius went on to explore other intense emotions in later choral works: the nostalgic *Songs of Sunset* (1906–7), the beguilingly sensuous *An Arabesque* (1911), the epic *Song of the High Hills* (1911–12) and the more controversial *Requiem* (1913–16), but *A Mass of Life* remains his most heroic choral masterpiece, unsurpassed in his output. ●

Jeremy Dibble is a Professor of Music at Durham University. The author of books on Parry, Stanford, Stainer and Hamilton Harty, he is a contributor to *Gramophone* and a regular consultant to recording companies and the BBC on British music of the 19th and 20th centuries.

Delius A Mass of Life
18 AUGUST

'A PROFOUNDLY
MAGICAL EXPERIENCE'

. ELLE

JOE HISAISHI AND ROYAL SHAKESPEARE COMPANY PRESENT
STUDIO GHIBLI'S

MY NEIGHBOUR TOTORO

in collaboration with NIPPON TV and IMPROBABLE
Adapted by TOM MORTON-SMITH from the feature animation by HAYAO MIYAZAKI
Music by JOE HISAISHI | Directed by PHELIM McDERMOTT

BOOK NOW ● totoroshow.com

GILLIAN LYNNE
THEATRE
LW THEATRES

Improbable

supported using public funding by
ARTS COUNCIL
ENGLAND

Portrait of Dmitry
Shostakovich by
Azerbaijani artist Tair
Salakhov (1928–2021)

PUPPET OR MASTER?

Dmitry Shostakovich is one of the most celebrated composers of the 20th century, yet his relationship with Stalin and status as a member of the Soviet elite remain contentious subjects. **MARINA FROLOVA-WALKER** reflects on his conflicting loyalties and the mix of ambition, success and terror that characterised his extraordinary career

Fifty years after his death Shostakovich remains a hugely influential figure. His symphonies – even the thorniest of them – still sell out concert halls. His *Suite for Variety Orchestra* is a cult classic. Novels and plays dramatising his life are still being written. You can buy Shostakovich T-shirts, mugs or posters featuring pictures of the composer: with a tennis racket, holding a pig or smoking a badly rolled cigarette. Looking glum, looking wicked or, in his younger days, looking like Harry Potter. Shostakovich has become a meme.

Born in St Petersburg in 1906, he seemed quite an ordinary boy until he reached the age of 9. This was when his mother, an able pianist, decided it was time he learnt a little about music. She couldn't have predicted the speed at which he would embrace this new language: within a few months he had memorised all the pieces of Tchaikovsky's *Album for*

the Young and then moved on to more difficult fare. As if this weren't enough, he wanted to compose his own pieces too. War and revolution surrounded him, so we find pieces entitled *The Soldier* and *Hymn to Freedom*. On the day of the Bolshevik Revolution in October 1917 Shostakovich, now 11, was out in the streets of Petrograd (as it was then called before becoming Leningrad in 1924) and saw a child die in the crossfire. A decade later this event also found its way into his music, in his Symphony No. 2, 'To October'. At the beginning of 1918 he performed his own *Funeral March for Victims of the Revolution* at his sister's school during a memorial event for two ministers of the Provisional Government killed in the revolutionary upheaval. Chaos, hope and tragedy were all part of his mental world at this early age.

Aged 12 he made the decision to become a musician. His early appearances as a composer and pianist were striking

enough to be recorded in various memoirs of the time. He is described coming on stage, badly dressed with broken glasses, his head at an awkward angle. This neatly sums up his public image as an adult too: though he managed to improve his appearance a little, Shostakovich was always awkward, seeming a little bit out of place.

He was soon a star student at the Petrograd Conservatory. His father died in 1922, a time when food and fuel were scarce, and it fell to young Dmitry to provide for the family. He found a very modern job in the cinema, becoming a successful piano accompanist for silent films – his mind as quick as his fingers. When Soviet sound films were introduced he wrote one of the earliest film scores, for 1929's *Noviy Vavilon* ('The New Babylon'). Throughout his career soundtracks formed a large part of his income, keeping him afloat even when he was in trouble for writing concert music that failed to align with Soviet-regime ideology. Some of his film music was for the best directors, but he wrote equally for popular and propaganda cinema.

After finishing at the cinema each night he would return home to work on his First Symphony. He wanted to show off his sophistication and original thinking, and especially that he had outgrown the rules taught at the conservatory. Though his professor, Maximilian Steinberg, found it all a bit too provocative and 'grotesque', the symphony was premiered, in 1926, to great acclaim, and the following year Bruno Walter conducted it in Berlin. Having achieved international fame, the 20-year-old decided he had better get to know his Western colleagues. He sought out scores and went to performances of music by leading modernists: Hindemith, Krenek, Schoenberg. He was particularly taken by Berg's opera *Wozzeck*, which was staged in Leningrad in 1927, with Berg present at the premiere. Modernist music was at this time still in circulation, almost unaffected by state censorship.

Shostakovich had a wicked sense of humour and a sharp tongue. He wrote hilarious letters to friends, full of sarcasm, self-irony and elaborate obscenities. All of this was put to good use in his absurdist opera *The Nose* (1927–8), about a bureaucrat who wakes up without a nose; later he finds the nose leading a grand life, and it refuses to come back. Shostakovich turned this unlikely story, by Gogol, into a brilliant piece of theatre with music that was very funny and often raucous. The timing, though, was not so good: by 1928

Joseph Stalin had begun to consolidate power within the Communist Party, introducing a programme of 'Socialism in one country'. There was no place for Western 'decadence', nor the irreverence and hijinks found in *The Nose*. If there were to be Soviet operas they should be conservative in their staging and music, with a heroic story to inspire workers and peasants. *The Nose* soon disappeared from the stage, as did Shostakovich's ballets *The Bolt* and *The Golden Age*.

66 Soviet composers were writing music that got blander year by year. But Shostakovich remained himself, in music stamped with his inner fury, despair and acerbic wit. 99

Shostakovich changed tack. His new opera *The Lady Macbeth of the Mtsensk District* was a serious one, about an oppressed woman striving for freedom in pre-Revolutionary Russia. This was a politically acceptable topic, despite the murderous heroine – after all, killing 'an enemy of the people' was a worthy undertaking in the Soviet Union of the early 1930s. It proved a great success. And, for the masses, Shostakovich also wrote a wildly popular song featured in the soundtrack to the film *The Counterplan*. Few would have disagreed that he was now the leading Soviet composer.

At least he was until 1936, when scandal made him a household name – even

in households that took no interest in music. Soviet culture had moved on since the premiere of *The Lady Macbeth*, and the opera was now long past its sell-by date. A performance attended by Stalin prompted wall-to-wall criticism in the Soviet press, most famously in an article for *Pravda* entitled 'This is Chaos, Not Music', which pilloried *The Lady Macbeth* as 'a stream of sounds that is … inharmonious and chaotic … a din of screeching and screaming'. Ostracised, Shostakovich was left without an income to feed his young family. The pressure to 'reform' was immense: he had to demonstrate a change not only in style but in 'ideology' too. His Fourth Symphony, nearly finished, was a complex, searching work of Mahlerian proportions and gargantuan orchestral forces that ended in muted tragedy. A performance in such a climate would have been a disaster. It somehow reached rehearsals until gradually the musicians, conductor, concert-hall administration and, finally, Shostakovich himself realised the project had to be abandoned.

Nineteen thirty-seven was the year of the Great Purge. Thousands of men and women – real or potential rivals and critics of Stalin – were removed from prominent positions and either transported to the Gulag (labour camps) or executed. Many of Shostakovich's own network were swept up in the terror. He insulated himself by focusing on a new symphony. Like the unperformed Fourth, this Fifth Symphony was a work of great depth, but this time with a narrative more accessible to the average listener. It even ended with a heroic, triumphant fanfare (although the extent to which this was sincere remains a subject of debate). Audiences felt that here was a tale of terrible difficulties overcome – one that every listener could take personally. There was a rapturous ovation at the premiere, and though the wheels of officialdom were slower to recognise the symphony's merit, it was eventually approved. Shostakovich had beaten all the odds and returned to pole position.

The travails of this 'reformed composer' intrigued many Soviet writers. Plays were created about Shostakovich's remarkable story. Reality brushed against fiction several times, most notably when Shostakovich himself was asked to write the music for one of these dramas. His colleagues were jealous: from this point on he seemed to get away with so much more than the rank and file of Soviet composers. His musical style was more challenging, his dissonances harsher, his moods more ambiguous. Aside from Shostakovich, Prokofiev and Khachaturian, Soviet composers were writing music that got blander year by year. Shostakovich remained himself, in music stamped with his inner fury, despair and acerbic wit. Even the Symphony No. 7, which was written during the Nazi siege of Leningrad and became an international symbol of Soviet resistance to Hitler, is no mere propaganda piece: it too has moments of mystery and irony.

The Seventh earned Shostakovich national-treasure status and rendered

him secure for six years. But his difficulties resurfaced in 1948 when, along with composers including Prokofiev and Khachaturian, he was denounced in the so-called Zhdanov Decree, which aimed to erase Western influences from Russian music and art. Shostakovich responded to this second blow with cynicism. Shrugging his shoulders, he gave the regime what it wanted, presenting Stalin with two gifts for his 70th birthday: a score for the hagiographical film *The Fall of Berlin*, and a celebration of a recent regime project in the oratorio *The Song of the Forests*. He soon rose back to the top of the pile, collecting his prizes as before – out of reach of his jealous colleagues.

After Stalin's death in 1953 Shostakovich entered calmer waters, becoming a respectable senior figure in Soviet society. There was greater artistic freedom in the late 1950s but it was the younger composers who took advantage of this: Shostakovich began to sound old-fashioned by comparison. Still, he managed to provoke the regime with his Symphony No. 13, set to poems that touched on the taboo theme of Soviet anti-Semitism: it disappeared from concert platforms. Alongside his mournful and lyrical late works, he continued writing satirical songs to the very end. Some of them are cryptically political, others are youthful, naughty or absurdist – the composer of *The Nose* was still alive deep inside the ailing, frail man.

In the West, too, Shostakovich was by now a household name. In the early 1940s

Stalin's body lying in state; the dictator died of a stroke on 5 March 1953, leading to a period of greater artistic freedom for Soviet composers such as Dmitry Shostakovich

„ЗАДАЧА СОСТОИТ В ТОМ, ЧТОБЫ ПОМОЧЬ СТАХАНОВЦАМ РАЗВЕРНУТЬ ДАЛЬШЕ СТАХАНОВСКОЕ ДВИЖЕНИЕ И РАСПРОСТРАНИТЬ ЕГО ВШИРЬ И ВГЛУБЬ НА ВСЕ ОБЛАСТИ И РАЙОНЫ СССР". И. СТАЛИН

ШИРЕ РЯДЫ СТАХАНОВЦЕВ!

'Wider, the ranks of Stakhanovites!': a Soviet propaganda poster depicting Communist Party leaders on a balcony overlooking a crowd of workers; the Stakhanovite movement, named after coal miner Alexei Stakhanov, was a Party-led campaign to increase worker productivity in the 1930s

he became a symbol of resistance against Hitler, photographed in a firefighter's helmet on the cover of *Time* magazine. In the late 1940s he was criticised for being a Soviet hack when he denounced Stravinsky at a so-called Peace Congress in New York – liberal intellectuals of the free world felt free to mock him. Late in the Cold War he was transformed again, this time into a resolute, if covert, dissident, thanks to the alleged memoir *Testimony* – a bestseller, but highly unreliable. Through to the present this has inspired countless documentaries, biographies and programme notes presenting a very partial picture of the composer as a victim of the regime.

But there is much more to Shostakovich than any of these stock images can offer, and he is, indeed, a difficult nut to crack. First, because he was a human with both vices and virtues, moments of courage and moments of cowardice. He had ambitions, but also inner torments, not to mention the simple need to earn money. He could stick to his principles, break them or even change them over time. Second, because it is difficult for us to see matters through his eyes as a member of the Soviet elite with chauffeur-driven cars, an exclusive apartment, holiday retreats in delightful locations, a command of the highest fees and a stream of fan letters. But it was a precarious elite, and he knew how it felt to lose everything in a single stroke, with humiliations and a fear of what might come next. And, lastly, we cannot fully grasp Shostakovich because he was unique: a genius who was

utterly devoted to music, working incessantly through the highs and lows of his outward life. The great mystery of how the world around him became the music in his mind will remain inaccessible to us.

Still, the music he left us is now ours. It can intrigue the intellect, touch the heart and cause the nerves to tingle. It can puzzle us, frighten us or make us laugh. It can take us to worlds we can't inhabit, but can also give us comfort and encouragement in our own pain. And, after we've experienced all of that, we can wear our Shostakovich T-shirt with pride. ●

Marina Frolova-Walker is Professor of Music History at the University of Cambridge and Fellow of Clare College, Cambridge. She is the author of *Russian Music and Nationalism from Glinka to Stalin* (Yale UP, 2007) and *Stalin's Music Prize: Soviet Culture and Politics* (Yale UP, 2016).

Suite for Variety Orchestra (arr. Atovmyan)
20 JULY

Symphony No. 13, 'Babi Yar'
15 AUGUST

Symphony No. 5 (performed from memory)
16 & 17 AUGUST

Chamber Symphony in C minor
31 AUGUST

The Lady Macbeth of the Mtsensk District
1 SEPTEMBER

Symphony No. 10
5 SEPTEMBER

Cello Concerto No. 1
10 SEPTEMBER

Festive Overture
13 SEPTEMBER

'THE BEST SHOW
IN LONDON'
DOMINIC CAVENDISH,
DAILY TELEGRAPH

BILLY PORTER   MARISHA WALLACE

CABARET

THE MUSICAL AT THE **KIT KAT CLUB**

book by
Joe Masteroff

music by
John Kander

lyrics by
Fred Ebb

based on the play by **John van Druten** and stories by **Christopher Isherwood**

WWW.KITKAT.CLUB

Photography by Dan Kennedy

Chapters Revisited

This summer Anoushka Shankar returns to the Proms, performing new arrangements of her recent trilogy of albums alongside conductor Robert Ames and the London Contemporary Orchestra. **BHANUJ KAPPAL** speaks to the composer and sitarist about the project, its role in her quest to 'de-exoticise' the sitar and her 20-year association with the Proms

On New Year's Day 2022, Anoushka Shankar sat in a little cafe in Goa scribbling in her diary. The 40-year-old composer and sitarist had spent the pandemic years in a creative rut. The trauma of the Covid-19 experience was too much – too big, still too raw – to process, but she felt the need to respond, to turn it into something profound. Weighed down by self-imposed expectation, she had gone around in circles. Now, in the fresh sunlight of a new year, she finally glimpsed a way out. 'Three chapters, three geographies,' she wrote, putting down the first blueprint for her next project. 'Three different producers. Show up with a blank slate.'

Those hastily scrawled notes would become the guiding principles for a new trilogy of 'mini-albums', culminating in a live performance with full orchestra at this year's Proms. The concept was simple: every few months she'd set up shop in a different studio with a new team of collaborators. Each location would represent one of the many places she called home – India, the UK and the USA. Instead of having an album-length concept already in place, she'd let herself be guided by the moment, writing smaller, simpler collections of songs that, she hoped, would eventually link up organically. 'I decided to show up to each session open to all possibilities, not

knowing what would happen,' says Shankar, who wrote most of the music in the studio with her collaborators. 'That freed me to just respond to where I was at emotionally, in that particular moment.'

With the idea of the cycle of morning till night emerging as the connecting thread, Shankar and her collaborators crafted distinct, Expressionist sound-worlds, moving from bittersweet winter afternoons in London to inky, expansive Californian nightscapes and, eventually, a euphoric post-rave Goan dawn. Her sitar weaves throughout, gleaming and shimmering in a sun-dappled haze one moment, assaulting the listener with waves of reverb-drenched sound the next. Along the way she crafts a new musical grammar for the instrument, drawing on everything from Philip Glass's Minimalism and the dreamy ambience of the Cocteau Twins to experimental electronica and even dance music.

The trilogy, then, is the high-water mark of Shankar's quest to reinvent the sitar as a secular, modern instrument. Or, as she puts it, to 'de-exoticise the sitar'. 'The second one picks up the sitar, a lot of people just instantly assume something deeply spiritual or really ancient is about to happen,' she says. 'And I love spirituality. But I also really started chafing against the idea that the instrument was synonymous with only one tradition or musical style. The sitar is not incense, or the Vedas or the 1960s, you know? An instrument is an instrument, and there are so many other ways you can play it and explore.'

Ever since 2005's *Rise* – her fourth album, but her first as a composer – Shankar has been pushing the sitar into new musical contexts, bringing it into conversation with contemporary genres (just as her father, the world-renowned sitarist Ravi Shankar, did during the latter half of the 20th century). 2011's *Traveller* saw her collaborate with Spanish singer-songwriter and producer Javier Limón, exploring links between flamenco and Hindustani classical music. On 2016's *Land of Gold*, an album about the global refugee crisis, her sitar rubs shoulders with glitched-out hip hop, found-sound samples and pop electronics. Then in 2020's *Love Letters* – written in the wake of her divorce – she pulled back from the complexity of her previous albums in favour of raw, stripped-back arrangements for cello, piano, sitar and voice, drawing back the curtain and letting the listeners into her inner world.

For her trilogy, Shankar mines similar emotional veins – the trauma of the pandemic, the challenges of single parenthood, the toll of a loved one's mental health struggles. On *Chapter I: Forever, For Now* – produced by Arooj Aftab (who also performs at the Proms this year) with composer Nils Frahm pitching in – the tender memory of a winter afternoon spent in the back garden of her London home with her two sons becomes a jumping-off point for an exploration of pain and the ephemerality of joy. It was while working on this album that she came up with the idea of tracing the journey through a day cycle,

◀ Anoushka Shankar, who returns to the Proms this summer for her fifth performance at the festival, having made her debut 20 years ago

Anoushka Shankar and Jules Buckley performing to an empty Royal Albert Hall during the 2020 Proms, which took place without a live audience owing to restrictions during the Covid-19 pandemic

symbolising different emotions and journeys – 'because that's so ingrained in my head from the raga system. The third song is in an evening raga, *Madhuvanti*, and it leads you into the sunset. So that set a template for the next album.'

In *Chapter II: How Dark It Is Before Dawn*, produced by Peter Raeburn, the anxieties of the day fade in the healing embrace of night. Best known for his film scores, Raeburn teases found-sound samples, synths and ambient electronics together to create expansive dreamscapes, with Shankar's sitar notes glistening like bioluminescent phytoplankton. 'I was thinking of the Pacific Ocean,' says Shankar, who went to high school in California. 'Every year I go back there and suddenly my hippie side feels validated and I become really positive. California just has this immensity to it that puts things into perspective.'

And then, on the recently released *Chapter III: We Return To Light*, Shankar and collaborators Sarathy Korwar and Alam Khan emerge energised and full of hope, repetitive percussion, looping sitar melodies and backwards sarod lines dancing with each other in joyous abandon. 'My visual image was entering the water in Goa after an all-night party,' says Shankar. 'That just felt like the ending, because there's a peacefulness to it. It's a homecoming in the true sense.'

With *Chapter III* now released, Shankar is looking ahead to the Proms, where she performs the trilogy with the London Contemporary Orchestra and conductor Robert Ames. She's already appeared at the festival on four occasions – the first with her father in 2005. Her most recent Proms performance, in 2020, was given to an empty Royal Albert Hall (a result of Covid-19 restrictions) alongside Jules Buckley, Gold Panda and Manu Delago. 'That was a weird, wonderful show,' she says. 'Another special one was in 2017, when we played the first ever live performance of *Passages*, my dad's album with Philip Glass. It was with the Britten Sinfonia and a full Indian ensemble – a really unusual and beautiful show.'

For this year's Prom she presents her trilogy in new arrangements by Ames. She's already been performing material from the first two chapters with her current band but is excited about the prospect of scaling things up from quintet to full orchestra. 'One of my favourite things about making music is watching songs evolve and change,' she says. 'I'm really curious about how some of it will work. Like when I play songs from *Chapter II* live, the whole audience is swimming in reverb. Will I still do it the same way, and have that enhanced by strings, or will that be a solo moment? And after two years of working on this trilogy, to finally have it all exist together in one place, that feels like an important conclusion to the journey for me.' ●

Bhanuj Kappal is a Mumbai-based culture writer whose work focuses on alternative music scenes across South Asia. He is a regular contributor to *Pitchfork*, the *Hindustan Times* and *GQ India*.

Anoushka Shankar: 'Chapters'
12 AUGUST

MVNICH OPERA FESTIVAL 150 YEARS

BAYERISCHE STAATSOPER

Gareth McConnell/Sorika, Meadow VI 2021

Munich Opera Festival
27 June–31 July 2025

慕尼黑歌剧节　　ミュンヘン歌劇祭

Global Partner der
Bayerischen Staatsoper

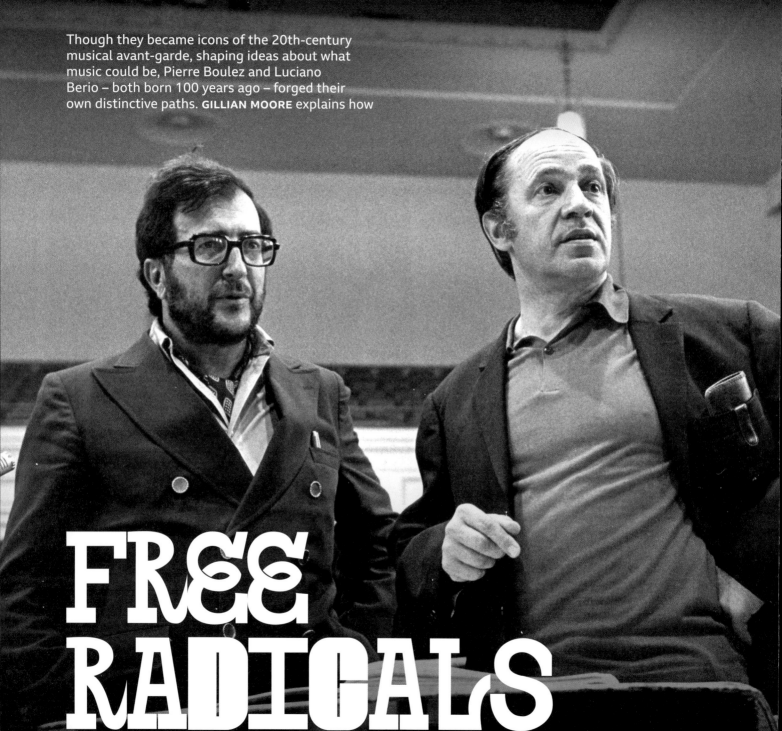

Though they became icons of the 20th-century musical avant-garde, shaping ideas about what music could be, Pierre Boulez and Luciano Berio – both born 100 years ago – forged their own distinctive paths. **GILLIAN MOORE** explains how

FREE RADICALS

A century ago, Pierre Boulez and Luciano Berio were born seven months and 230 miles apart. Boulez came into the world in Montbrison, a town close to Lyon, known for a variety of creamy blue cheese. Berio was born in Oneglia, on Italy's Ligurian coast, famous for olive oil and pasta. Both men were to become giants of music in the second half of the 20th century. The two Bs had much in common: they were leaders in that generation of composers who reshaped music after the Second World War – Stockhausen, Ligeti, Xenakis among them – and who gathered at the Darmstadt summer school. Boulez and Berio were both also performers, conductors and thinkers, and they became cultural movers and shakers, founding ensembles, running festivals and instituting electronic music studios. Their paths crossed frequently, they dedicated works to each other and presented each other's music. And yet they differed in their tastes and personalities, and in their music. You would never mistake the work of one B for that of the other.

Music was not part of Boulez's background. His father was an engineer but his mother sent all three of her children to piano lessons. Pierre showed particular aptitude, and on moving to a more advanced teacher in nearby Saint-Étienne he had a crucial encounter with

◀ Rebels with a cause: Luciano Berio and Pierre Boulez at a recording session in 1974

the seductive sound-world of Debussy. Pierre initially studied Advanced Mathematics in Lyon, feeding his passion for music in parallel. He went to orchestral concerts and operas. Eventually the 18-year-old Boulez chose music and found his way to the Conservatoire in wartime Paris. In the class of Olivier Messiaen he studied recent works such as Stravinsky's ballet *The Rite of Spring* and Debussy's opera *Pelléas and Mélisande*, as well as Monteverdi, Schumann, Bartók and Ravel. At the same time he was slipping off to the Musée Guimet and the Musée de l'Homme in Paris to study the music of Japan, Bali, India, China and Africa, attracted not only by its sound but also by the fact that it forced him to think about time in a different way.

By contrast, for Luciano Berio, there was never any doubt that music would be his life. 'I never had to decide,' he said simply. Luciano came from a musical dynasty in Oneglia; his father and grandfather were composers and organists. He once described childhood memories of falling asleep to the sound of Beethoven, Schubert and Brahms during his father's chamber music evenings. He imbibed opera and song and remembers listening as a 13-year-old to Puccini's *La bohème* on the radio; he was unable to control his tears. The Darmstadt composers are said to have wanted to eradicate the musical past in order to invent a brave new musical world. For Berio, although he was as dedicated an avant-gardist as the rest of them, rejecting the past was not an option. He welcomed the whole of music

into his works, whether Monteverdi, Schubert, Donizetti, Boccherini or Mahler. And he embraced popular culture too: folk songs, The Beatles, the cabaret of Kurt Weill. He was an Italian, after all – he loved a good tune.

The young Pierre Boulez, though, was given to polemical confrontation with musical history. When Arnold Schoenberg died in 1951, Boulez penned an article entitled 'Schoenberg Is Dead', suggesting, with the trenchant certainty of a 26-year-old, that not only was Schoenberg physically dead, but so were his ideas – 'echoes of a dead world', a 'classico-romantic' dead end. As Boulez's attitude to the music of the past evolved, he recognised Wagner as part of a sweep of musical history that led to his own music and that of his contemporaries. And, as Music Director in the 1970s of both the New York Philharmonic and the BBC Symphony Orchestra, Boulez established a new standard for the performance of early 20th-century music: Bartók, Stravinsky, Berg, Janáček, Debussy, Ravel – and even Schoenberg.

There's no question that Boulez's breakthrough piece, *Le marteau sans maître* ('The Hammer without a Master', 1953–5), feels like something utterly fresh. For a start, there's the use of the sung texts by René Char, hero of the French Resistance and conjurer of startling, Surrealist images: a corpse in a basket, a pair of eyes in a forest looking for a head, a dream on the point of a knife in Peru. The structure of the work is subtly revolutionary. Boulez only uses

Pierre Boulez at a rehearsal in 2009 at IRCAM, the computer-music research centre he instituted in Paris in 1977

Luciano Berio in his study in Radicondoli, Siena, 1995

those Char texts in four of the nine short movements. The other five foreshadow, echo or provide commentary on the poems. It's almost as if he is trying to play tricks with time, to make it move in different directions – perhaps something he learnt from the Asian and African music he'd studied in the mid-1940s. The actual sound of the piece was also new, thanks to its scoring for seven-piece ensemble: alto voice, alto flute, viola, guitar and an array of tuned and untuned percussion. The sound has something sensuous about it. Yes, it could be the spikier offspring of the shimmer and seductiveness of Debussy or Ravel, but it also suggests more distant sounds – from Japan, India, China, Bali – heard through the filter of European modernism. Two decades later Boulez's *Rituel: in memoriam Bruno Maderna* (1974–5) was a heartfelt tribute to his friend and fellow figure of the Darmstadt generation, who had died at 53 of lung cancer. *Rituel* is the piece most audibly drawn from Asian music, a 'litany for an imaginary ceremonial', Boulez said, in which a repeating drum beat and reedy, mouth-organ-like chords suggest a Japanese gagaku orchestra. But you could also hear it as a late 20th-century take on a Mahler funeral march: repeating, solemn, inexorable.

Maderna was also close to Berio and together, in 1955, they founded Italy's first electronic music studio at the Milan headquarters of RAI, the Italian national broadcaster. Berio's then wife, the American-Armenian mezzo-soprano Cathy Berberian, was an important member of the team of artists around the studio, with her almost superhuman vocal dexterity. Berio's first major work in the studio was *Thema (Omaggio a Joyce)* (1958), a whole world of sound and meaning using only Berberian's voice. She selected and performed extracts from Joyce's *Ulysses*, which were then manipulated with tape techniques and oscillators: atomising, layering and transforming her voice, exploding the words and music into new realms.

It was almost two decades later that Boulez opened the computer-music research centre IRCAM in Paris. His own major IRCAM work was *Répons* (1980–84), in which live musicians and electronic sounds respond to each other to create a thrilling immersive experience. Boulez appointed Berio as Director of Electroacoustic music at IRCAM and dedicated another important electronic work to him: *Dialogue de l'ombre double* ('Dialogue of the Double Shadow', 1982–5). A solo clarinettist dialogues with their own pre-recorded musical shadow, which moves around the space via a group of speakers while the clarinet sounds are transformed by live electronics in a kind of sonic hall of mirrors.

Cathy Berberian continued to be an important collaborator of Berio's until her early death in 1983. The most celebrated piece on which they worked together is the masterly *Folk Songs* from 1964. The 11 songs, written for Berberian and a small instrumental ensemble, are from America, Armenia, France, Sardinia, Sicily and Azerbaijan. Here, Berio wanted to explore the connections between folk traditions and contemporary art music. While most of the songs are from genuine folk sources, the American songs were written in a folk style by the early 20th-century composer and singer John Jacob Niles; the two Italian songs ('La donna ideale' and 'Ballo') were newly composed by Berio (but as if he were passing them off as ancient) and the 'Azerbaijan Love Song' is a popular song transcribed by Berberian from a 78 rpm record. Berio linked the songs with a kind of instrumental connective tissue that leads us from one to the next.

> ❝ Music was not part of Boulez's background … By contrast, there was never any doubt for Luciano Berio that music would be his life. ❞

In his most famous piece, *Sinfonia* (1968–9) for large orchestra and amplified voices, Berio is at his most daring in terms of sweeping up what seems like the entire history of Western music. At the same time, *Sinfonia* is that rare thing: a piece of concert music that confronts the very moment in history in which it was created; it documents the excitement, the pain and confusion of being alive in that turbulent year when young people took to the streets of Paris to protest, Martin Luther King Jr and Robert F. Kennedy were assassinated and the social order was questioned. Right from the get-go, when we hear a lush, close-miked chord from the Swingle Singers (who made the

first recording), we know where we are – it's a signature sound of the 1960s. While Berio was writing *Sinfonia*, news came of the assassination of Martin Luther King Jr. So the second movement becomes a tiny, devastating requiem made entirely from the syllables of King's name. The shimmering, simple music seems almost frozen with grief, so it's all the more shocking when we are tumbled out of it and into the torrents of the famous third movement. The scherzo of Mahler's 'Resurrection' Symphony (No. 2), Berio said, courses through this movement like a mighty river, on which flotsam and jetsam of words and music rush past. We hear texts from Beckett and slogans shouted by the student demonstrators at the Paris barricades in May 1968; snatches of music from Stravinsky's *The Rite of Spring*, Beethoven's 'Pastoral' Symphony (No. 6), Ravel's *La valse*, Richard Strauss's *Der Rosenkavalier*. It could be a modish pop-art sonic collage. In fact it's a thrilling, moving and profound meditation on the past and the present, on human endeavour, on fear and exhilaration – as well as being just a wonderful noise.

Boulez admired *Sinfonia*; he made a recording of it and, near the end of his life, chose it as one of his top 10 20th-century pieces, partly because, as he said, 'I could never have written it myself'. If Boulez couldn't let everything into his own music in the way that Berio could, the two Bs certainly did share a broad vision of what a life in music could be. Just weeks before Berio died in 2003,

I interviewed him on the stage of the Accademia Nazionale di Santa Cecilia in Rome, where he was Artistic Director. We conducted the interview, then had a planning meeting for the forthcoming London festival of his music and after that he went into a union meeting to discuss staffing – all this when he was clearly very sick. During our interview he said: 'I never say I'm a composer. I'm a musician; I compose, conduct, teach, administrate, write. Being a musician is a very wide landscape to inhabit.' And that, for sure, could be said of both of them. ●

Gillian Moore is Artistic Associate of London's Southbank Centre and was Artistic Director of the London Sinfonietta (1998–2006). She is the author of *The Rite of Spring: The Music of Modernity* (Apollo, 2019) and was appointed CBE in 2018.

Boulez Dialogue de l'ombre double
Berio Sequenza V; Recital I (for Cathy)
23 JULY

Boulez Le marteau sans maître
GATESHEAD • 27 JULY

Berio Sinfonia
1 AUGUST

Boulez Rituel: in memoriam Bruno Maderna
4 AUGUST

Berio Rendering
23 AUGUST

Berio Folk Songs
BRISTOL • 24 AUGUST

Discover …

GEORGE FRIDERIC HANDEL'S
Alexander's Feast

ALEXANDRA COGHLAN considers the dramatic work that spearheaded the fashion for English oratorio, and which expounds music's ability to stir the soul

The first performance of Handel's *Alexander's Feast* in February 1736 wasn't just the premiere of a new work, it was the birth of a new genre. With it Handel offered his audience the first truly English oratorio. Opera's star was on the wane, and Handel responded by giving the public exactly what they wanted, even if they didn't yet know it themselves.

'Never was … so numerous and splendid an audience at any theatre in London,' reported the London *Daily Post*. A critical, financial and popular success, *Alexander's Feast* was revived more frequently than almost any other piece by Handel during his lifetime. Just two years after its premiere, a statue of the composer – complete with *Alexander* score in hand – would take its place in London's Vauxhall Gardens, cementing Handel's adoption as an honorary Englishman.

Aptly, the plot of *Alexander's Feast* hinges on the power of music. We join the story during a victory banquet: Alexander the Great has conquered Persia. But while Alexander is all-powerful on the battlefield, musician Timotheus tests art's rival strength, turning the warrior-king into a slave to emotion with his songs and finally inciting him to burn Persepolis to the ground – vengeance for the many Greek dead.

This was Handel's first time setting truly great English poetry, and John Dryden's verse seems to have thrown down the gauntlet, challenging the composer to greater invention, innovation and sheer musical beauty than ever before. 'It is next to an improbability,' Handel's librettist-adaptor Newburgh Hamilton wrote, 'to offer the world anything … more perfect than the united labours … of a Dryden and a Handel.'

Dryden's poem may be descriptive rather than dramatic, but Handel pushes drama to the fore, defying musical conventions for maximum impact. The composer keeps the drama moving forward in a sequence of almost symphonic musical arcs, creating an unusually organic, urgent flow of action.

One of Handel's richest scores, *Alexander's Feast* incorporates recorders, bassoons, trumpets and horns into the orchestra, varies the accompanying continuo (secondary) group for subtle textural difference, and sets the voices in duet with solo cello and violin. The music creates a vivid psychological portrait of Alexander, the 'vanquish'd victor' – a paradox mirrored in Handel's deft sonic characterisation. As the cello that opens 'Softly sweet, in Lydian measures' weaves around us in beguiling arabesques of melody, we find ourselves in Alexander's seat: compelled to surrender to Timotheus' unrelenting manipulation and to the power of music. ●

Alexandra Coghlan is a music journalist and critic who contributes regularly to *The Spectator*, *Prospect*, *The Independent*, *Gramophone* and *Opera* magazine; she is the author of *Carols from King's* (Ebury, 2016).

Handel Alexander's Feast
30 AUGUST

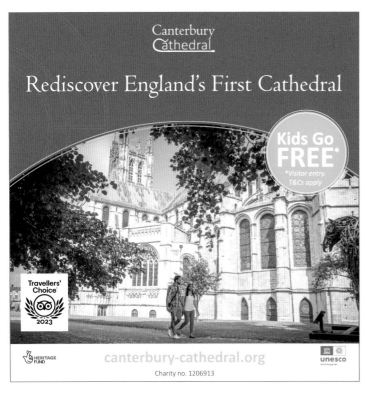

ENESCU
FESTIVAL

George Enescu International Festival

24.08 · 21.09.2025

Bucharest, the World's Capital of Classical Music.

ROMÂNIA

Event held under the High Patronage of the President of Romania

PREȘEDINTELE ROMÂNIEI

GUVERNUL ROMÂNIEI

MINISTERUL CULTURII

Cultural Project financed by the Romanian Government through the Ministry of Culture

artexim

America Sings!

JANUARY–APRIL 2026

For the 250th anniversary of the United States, we celebrate the rich range of
American voices in the beautiful winter paradise of Tucson, Arizona.

Highlights of the 2026 festival include the world premiere of a Festival-commissioned song cycle by the exciting
composer Gregory Spears. His latest opera, *The Righteous*, premiered in 2024 at Santa Fe Opera with
Jennifer Johnson Cano who will debut this new song cycle in recital in April 2026.

JAMIE BARTON

ANGELA BROWER

JENNIFER JOHNSON CANO

D. JEROME

WILL LIVERMAN

GREGORY SPEARS

DAVÓNE TINES

Recitals | Opera | Symphony | Jazz | Dance | Classical Guitar | Chamber Music | Choral Music | Theater | Early Music

TUCSON DESERT SONG FESTIVAL

TucsonSongFest.org

Jeannette Jung Segel, President
Julia Pernet, Vice President
Juliana Osinchuk, Artistic Advisory

Artists subject to change

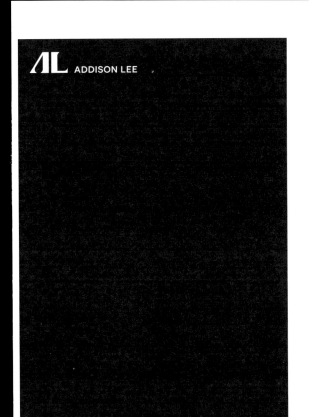

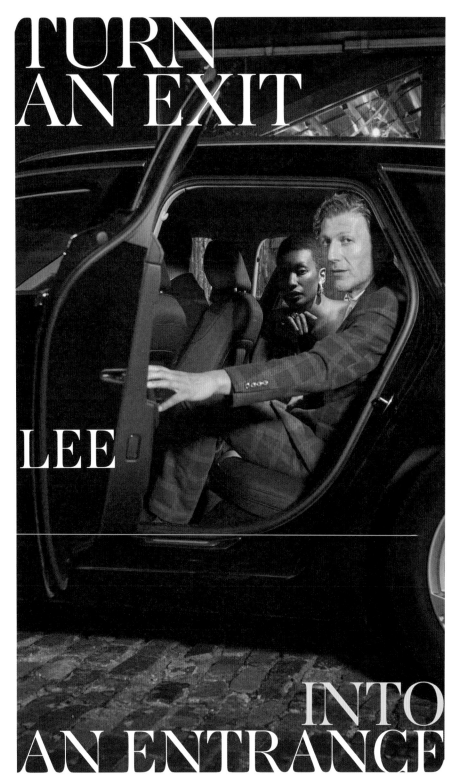

The Curse of the Ninth

Many contenders have entered the zone of symphony-writing in the game of musical history but for a conspicuous few – Beethoven, Bruckner and Dvořák among them – the journey ended with the number nine. **OLIVIA GIOVETTI** investigates the lore and checks out the leaderboards

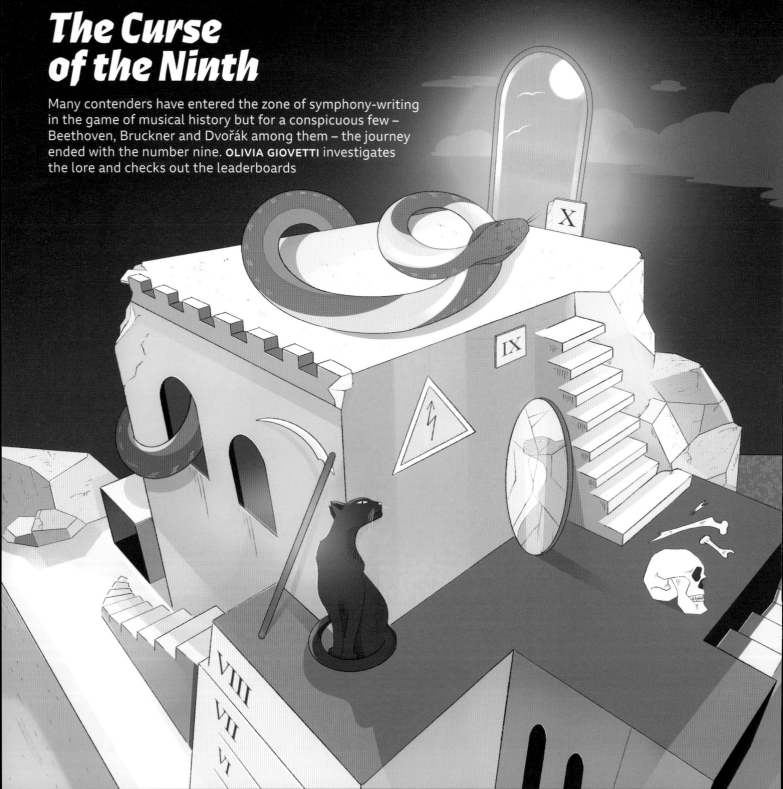

A spectre has been haunting composers – the spectre of the Ninth Symphony. A number of our most celebrated composers died after writing their ninth symphony but before completing their 10th. Beethoven, Bruckner, Dvořák, Vaughan Williams and Schnittke all fell prey to the Curse of the Ninth.

This pattern haunted Gustav Mahler who, according to his wife Alma, 'dreaded' the prospect of crossing this musical Rubicon. His fear originated with Beethoven and Bruckner. The fact that neither of these made it past their ninth became a kind of shibboleth for him. 'It was a superstition of Mahler's that no great writer of symphonies got beyond his ninth,' Alma wrote.

Mahler tried to hoodwink fate. When he came to write his ninth symphony, instead of naming it so, he gave it the title *Das Lied von der Erde* and cast it as an orchestral song-cycle. Later, while working on what he would call his Ninth, he told Alma. 'Actually, of course, it's the Tenth because *Das Lied von der Erde* was really the Ninth.' When he then began work on his 10th Symphony, he sighed with relief: 'Now the danger is past.' Except it wasn't: when Mahler died, he left his 10th unfinished. Critic Tim Ashley has described this work as 'a legendary, if futile, attempt to ward off mortality'.

◀ Next-level challenge: for a surprising number of ill-fated composers, finishing their ninth symphony has spelled 'game over'

The Curse of the Ninth was the classical precursor to the 27 Club – that informal collective of pop musicians, from Jimi Hendrix to Kurt Cobain to Amy Winehouse – who all died at 27. 'It seems that the ninth is a limit. He who wants to go beyond it must pass away,' wrote Arnold Schoenberg. 'Those who have written a ninth stood too close to the hereafter.' A devotee of numerology, Schoenberg would have known that, as the last single digit, the number represents an end point. Had he lived to see the 27 Club take form he might have pointed out that 27 is a multiple of nine.

Schoenberg helped to propagate the Curse of the Ninth, to the point that even sceptics tread carefully: 'You get nervous … ninth symphony, what kind of silly jinx is that?' composer Philip Glass said shortly before the 2012 premiere of his own Ninth. 'But I wasn't going to wait to find out.' He completed his 10th Symphony less than two months after his Ninth.

But does the curse actually hold water? Plenty of composers have entered symphonic double digits *(see 'Beyond the Ninth', overleaf)*, while even in Mahler's day the symphony was becoming less of a concern as composers explored other musical forms. Richard Strauss, like Berlioz and Liszt before him, focused more on tone-poems. Verdi and Wagner were following in the footsteps of Rossini and Donizetti in busying themselves with operas. Schoenberg himself never wrote a numbered symphony for full orchestra (nor did Chopin, Bartók, Debussy, Gershwin or Ravel).

If the number nine stood out to Mahler, it was in part because few other composers in his time were as dedicated to the symphonic cause. Speaking at an American Symphony Orchestra League meeting in 1980, Leonard Bernstein noted that there had been significant contributions to the genre since Mahler (Sibelius, Copland and Prokofiev among them), but that Stravinsky's *Symphony in Three Movements* was 'the last really great symphony, in the broad classical sense of the term'. By the 20th century composers had many more genres to work with and, often, less access to a full orchestra.

The greater curse for many composers seems to be Beethoven's Ninth, in and of itself. 'Who would be able to do anything after Beethoven?' wondered Schubert, who himself died just a few weeks after starting his 10th Symphony. Over a century later, British composer George Lloyd echoed the sentiment: 'There are other very good Number Fives and Number Threes, for instance, but how can one possibly have the temerity of trying to write another Ninth Symphony?'

Beethoven's Ninth sits at the crossroads of personal and political crisis and renewal. Though he wrote his 'Heiligenstadt Testament' 22 years before the symphony's 1824 premiere, its shadow looms large over the work. In this 1802 letter, Beethoven described his growing deafness and the despair to which it had driven him: 'O you men who think or say that I am malevolent, stubborn or misanthropic, how greatly do you wrong me,' he begins. 'You do not

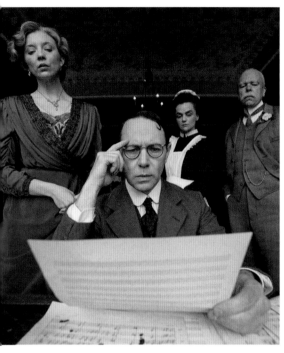

Reece Shearsmith with *(left to right)* Natalie Dormer, Hayley Squires and Steve Pemberton in the gothic-Edwardian 'Curse of the Ninth', an episode from the ninth – and final! – series of the BBC's dark-comedy anthology *Inside No. 9*; as one of the characters observes: 'Beethoven, Dvořák, Schubert, Bruckner. After the Ninth, they all went from composing to decomposing.'

know the secret cause that makes me seem that way.' He mirrors this silent agitation in the opening of his Ninth: a tremolo of strings set against the drone of horns, a flicker of melody that soon blazes into a full orchestral bellow. Following a push–pull of order and chaos, of expression and repression, his Ninth ends in zeal and humanity, as if Beethoven were triumphing over his own demons – the outer world that thinks him malevolent and the secret, inner causes of his seeming so. Yet his Ninth is not just his own victory, but also one for humanity. 'Join in one embrace, you millions,' the chorus sings. 'Share this kiss with all the world.'

Bruckner's admiration for Beethoven was so extreme that, in 1888, he forced his way into the exhumation of his hero's grave in order to hold the composer's skull. He likewise borrowed some of the bones of Beethoven's Ninth for his own Ninth Symphony, including the key of D minor and a reordering of movements that places the Scherzo (typically a third movement) as the second. He was acutely aware of his own mortality when he began working on the symphony in earnest in 1891, amid attacks of pneumonia, heart disease, depression and religious mania. He dedicated the work 'to the beloved God'. It was a move his physician described as a contract with the creator in order to vouchsafe the piece's completion: 'Should he die earlier, then it is God's own fault if He receives an incomplete work.'

In the end, God did receive an incomplete work: Bruckner died while working on

the Finale. Bruckner's Ninth isn't the culmination of personal or political struggle. It's instead a sort of musical version of the prayer journals the composer kept, turned up to 11. Even the silences – two deliberate full-orchestral rests in the first movement – are roaring. This is Bruckner's final entry in his spiritual bookkeeping, and he is determined to make everything add up. That comes across in the third movement, which he titled 'Farewell to Life'. The pained opening bars soon resolve into lyrical serenity. As a dyed-in-the-wool Catholic, Bruckner knew that death wasn't an end, it was a homecoming.

Of the three Ninths featured in this year's Proms, the one that manages to stray furthest from the Curse is Dvořák's. Written and premiered in 1893, 'From the New World' was completed over a decade before the Czech composer's death at the age of 62, and shows very little trace of finality. He was just reaching the height of his career, dividing his time between Europe and New York (where he had been made the head of the National Conservatory of Music in America) when the New York Philharmonic commissioned the symphony.

Aware that America was still trying to shape its musical identity, Dvořák used his Ninth to showcase what he had learnt of Black spirituals and Native American songs (as authentically as he had heard either), positioning both as the future of American music. When critics later suggested that Dvořák himself had 'invented' American music, he had to smirk. 'It seems that I have got them all confused.' He was not creating the 'new world' that became the nickname of his symphony, but rather reporting from it.

Dvořák may have been spared the curse on a technicality: he himself didn't realise that 'From the New World' was his ninth symphony. He lost the score for his First Symphony after he had sent the autograph manuscript to a competition and never received it back. Considering the work permanently gone, he began his subsequent symphonies from No. 1 again, cataloguing 'From the New World' as his eighth. The order was only straightened out long after Dvořák's death, when his scores were properly dated following the discovery of his long-lost First Symphony in a private collection.

Perhaps, also, Dvořák was too pragmatic to believe any musical Rubicon to be impassable. The real curse, as we discover in another of his best-known works, is human nature. That idea comes from *Rusalka*, premiered in 1901. It was his ninth opera. ●

Olivia Giovetti has written about music and culture for the BBC, *Financial Times*, *London Review of Books* and *Washington Post*, and has written programme notes for the New York Philharmonic, Glyndebourne, Edinburgh International Festival and Scottish Opera. She lives in Berlin.

Dvořák Symphony No. 9, 'From the New World'
7 AUGUST

Beethoven Symphony No. 9, 'Choral'
21 AUGUST

Bruckner Symphony No. 9
8 SEPTEMBER

Beyond the Ninth

The composers who triumphed over the Curse.

There are more composers who can debunk the Curse of the Ninth than there are who can support it. Both Hans Werner Henze and Peter Maxwell Davies completed 10 symphonies well before their deaths. We could even consider Schnittke as having 10 complete symphonies to his name: Nos. 1–9 (plus his student work now numbered '0'). Mozart completed 41 symphonies over his 35 years.

Much more industrious was Joseph Haydn, who wrote 104 numbered symphonies (his brother Michael was a comparative slouch, managing a meagre 41). As with Mozart, many of Joseph Haydn's late symphonies are his best-known, most notably his 'London' cycle (Nos. 93–104).

The undisputed champion, however, is Finnish conductor-composer Leif Segerstam *(pictured above)*, who died last October with 371 symphonies to his name. A larger-than-life figure in all respects, Segerstam beat the Curse of the Ninth 41 times over, comparing their profusion to that of male reproductive cells. Like sperm, he joked, 'there must be a huge number of them in order for some to survive'.

Many critics have posited that the symphony died with Mahler, but that didn't preclude symphonic efforts in the 20th and 21st centuries. American Alan Hovhaness, a friend of John Cage, wrote 67; the subtitle of his 11th is a subtle nod to Beethoven's Ninth: 'All Men Are Brothers'. Mieczysław Weinberg and Nikolai Myaskovsky, contemporaries of Shostakovich, wrote 25 and 27 symphonies respectively. Havergal Brian, whose massive No. 1 ('The Gothic') was heard at the Proms in 2011, penned 32 – of which 21 were written after he turned 70.

Among the most famous symphonists after 1945 was Shostakovich, whose own Ninth coincided with the end of the Second World War and became a celebration of Soviet victory over the Nazis. 'Musicians will like to play it, and critics will delight in blasting it,' Shostakovich quipped before the work's premiere, and while some critics dismissed the work as childish and unserious, others saw in its playful energy the spirit of Mozart.

Shostakovich's final symphony, the 15th, was premiered in 1972, less than four years before his death, at a time when the form was enjoying a healthy run. His contemporary, Darius Milhaud (a member of the French group of composers known as Les Six) authored 12 between 1939 and 1962. Brazilian composer Heitor Villa-Lobos also wrote a dozen, completing the last on his 70th birthday in 1957. Henry Cowell premiered his 20th Symphony in 1965.

The list of female composers with a significant catalogue of symphonies is, not surprisingly, shorter. However, American composer Julia Perry (1924–79, a student in Paris of Nadia Boulanger) wrote 12. Another American, Gloria Coates (1933–2023) completed 16; and Alla Pavlova – born in Soviet Ukraine but now living in New York – currently has 11 to her name.

Olivia Giovetti

Tied Brides

Opera is littered with tragic heroines who have endured rejection, betrayal and self-sacrifice. **FIONA MADDOCKS** delves into the lives of four 20th-century characters trapped in coercive relationships or desperate circumstances, and who find their own paths to freedom or redemption

A drama of abstract ideas, or a battle between a man and a woman; a tragedy of abuse and violence or of obstinate curiosity? Béla Bartók's *Duke Bluebeard's Castle*, a thrilling masterpiece of the early 20th century, is all these things. The more you encounter this one-act opera, which has a vast orchestra and only two characters, the more you are drawn into its tenacious web. The text (by Béla Balázs) proceeds with a set of questions – apparently answered, yet leaving us none the wiser – while the subtle and majestic orchestra – complete with multiple woodwind and brass, two harps, celesta and organ – provides its own, often contradictory narrative, its stark beauty at odds with the unfolding mood of dread.

First performed at the State Opera House, Budapest in 1918, *Bluebeard* has a clear plot, loosely based on Charles Perrault's 17th-century fairy tale, but far more menacing than the original: Duke Bluebeard (bass-baritone) takes his new wife, Judith (mezzo-soprano), to his castle hidden deep in a forest. She wants to know what lies behind each of seven locked doors. He refuses to say. She insists. He yields. She, oddly fearless and brave, but also under her husband's inexplicable spell, takes the terrible consequences. In Bartók's opera there is no redemption, only

◀ Sergey (Brandon Jovanovich) and Katerina (Evgenia Muraveva) wrestle in the Salzburg Festival's 2017 production of Shostakovich's *The Lady Macbeth of the Mtsensk District*, directed by Andreas Kriegenburg

darkness, mystery, doom. The name 'Bluebeard' is synonymous with a man who murders one wife and moves on to the next, but his reasons are enigmatic, his profound sadness ever apparent.

Some see the opera as a phantasmagorical dream, in which the controlling forces of obsession, violence and rejection circle and swoop around the protagonists like bats at dusk. Shaped by the new thinking of Sigmund Freud (whose game-changing *The Interpretation of Dreams* was published in 1900), Bluebeard's windowless castle becomes the central character, the human soul itself. Its walls and garden bleed and weep. The spoken Prologue asks, provocatively: 'Are we outside or inside?' The desire of lovers to know everything about each other is the stuff of all romance. As Shakespeare's Benedick tells Beatrice in *Much Ado About Nothing*, 'I will live in thy heart, die in thy lap, and be buried in thy eyes'. Judith wants to know all. Bluebeard resists her probings: 'You may look, but ask no questions', or 'Judith, love me, do not ask me'. An early director of the opera – the Austrian, Ernst Lert (1883–1955), who staged it in Frankfurt in 1922 – summed up his view of the piece. 'What my mind heard was a surrealist reality – what my mind saw looked like a moving kaleidoscope of exuberant shapes in challenging colours.' Struggling to work out how to stage it, Lert placed it in a gloomy void: the human psyche, with all its untellable secrets and neuroses, its desires and terrors, set to Bartók's mesmerising, unforgettable music.

While *Duke Bluebeard's Castle* inhabits a shadowy, interior world, Dmitry Shostakovich's *The Lady Macbeth of the Mtsensk District* (1930–32) is the opposite: extrovert, noisy, audacious, satirical, raucous, rude, outrageous *(see also 'Puppet or Master?', pages 58–62)*. In this real, physical world, mushrooms, rat poison, raunchy sex and a drunken priest appear. Bursting with musical allusion and parody, the score embraces a potpourri of styles, complete with brass band interlude and expansive choruses. The young composer was at the peak of his powers in Stalin's Soviet Union. Much was expected of this second opera (the first had been *The Nose*, in 1930). Instead, a disaster occurred that would crush Shostakovich's desire to create opera. In one of the most famous condemnations in all music, *The Lady Macbeth* – despite its successful premiere in 1934 – was castigated in the official newspaper, *Pravda*, as 'This is Chaos, Not Music', and banned in the Soviet Union until 1961. Shostakovich produced a new, tamer version, *Katerina Ismailova* (named after the lead character), but today the edgier original is back in the mainstream repertoire, and is the version heard at the Proms this summer.

Based on a short story by Nikolai Leskov, *The Lady Macbeth* tells of a bored young wife, Katerina, who falls in love with one of her husband's workers and, in a plot that lurches from comedy to horror, turns murderer – a tale of a typical 'quiet Russian family' in the provinces, as Shostakovich once, ironically, noted. Desolation and loneliness, and a wish to live a fuller life,

Secrets and wives: Clive Bayley as the treacherous Duke Bluebeard and Michaela Martens as Judith (his fourth bride) in English National Opera's 2009 production of Bartók's *Duke Bluebeard's Castle*, directed by Daniel Kramer

lead Katerina into a spiral of degradation, lies and crime. For all her misdeeds, she alone evokes pathos. Her menfolk have no redeeming features. In seeking a better, more rewarding existence, answering her own, questing spirit, she merely creates an inescapable hell for herself. With its fast-moving action and relentless musical variety, *The Lady Macbeth* has all the intensity of a thriller.

Two other 20th-century operas featured at this season's Proms. Both feature women tormented by circumstance: Giacomo Puccini's *Suor Angelica* (one of the three operas of *Il trittico*, premiered in 1918) and Richard Strauss's *Die Frau ohne Schatten*. In Puccini's short, heart-breaking work, a young noblewoman has renounced a worldly life to become a nun (the title's Sister Angelica). Attempting to suppress her longings, and harbouring a secret, she hopes for a visit from her family to hear news of her illegitimate son. Instead of giving her comfort, and despite her efforts, the secluded life with other women merely accentuates her loss. Her aunt, the Princess, visits, cruelly reminding Angelica of the shame she has brought on the family. The child, she tells her niece, is dead. Angelica is devastated, eventually finding spiritual redemption in the only way left to her.

Die Frau ohne Schatten ('The Woman without a Shadow'), premiered at the Vienna State Opera in 1919, surely counts as one of the most baffling, yet most musically beguiling and ambitious collaborations between Strauss and the poet Hugo von Hofmannsthal. The story,

a grown-up fairy tale with two couples at its heart, combines mythical and real, fantasy and human anguish. The Empress (the 'Frau' of the opera's title) starts life as a gazelle, and becomes human in form on marriage to the Emperor of the South Eastern Isles, but she has no shadow. This absence reflects her inability to have children. She persuades the wife of Barak, the dyer, to sell her shadow. *Die Frau* is sometimes referred to as an opera about childbearing. It is far more than that: a work about rebuilding, humanity, compassion. Strauss, near the end of his life, and always above all a practical musician, wanted to bring the best parts of his score to a concert audience. He made his single-movement Symphonic Fantasy in 1947. The orchestra, though smaller than for the opera, features a glittering array of percussion, celesta, organ, two harps and plenty more. Listen out for the work's grand, climactic finale, which should fill the Royal Albert Hall. Don't miss it. ●

Fiona Maddocks is the classical music critic of *The Observer* and author of *Hildegard of Bingen: The Woman of Her Age* (2013), *Music for Life: 100 Works to Carry You Through* (2018), the conversation diary *Harrison Birtwistle: Wild Tracks* (2014) and *Goodbye Russia: Rachmaninoff in Exile* (2023, all Faber).

Bartók Duke Bluebeard's Castle
6 AUGUST

Strauss Die Frau ohne Schatten – Symphonic Fantasy; **Puccini** Suor Angelica
19 AUGUST

Shostakovich The Lady Macbeth of the Mtsensk District
1 SEPTEMBER

Discover …

GUSTAV MAHLER'S

Das klagende Lied

STEPHEN JOHNSON on the great symphonic composer's early choral work that marries expressive power with the world of dark fairy tales

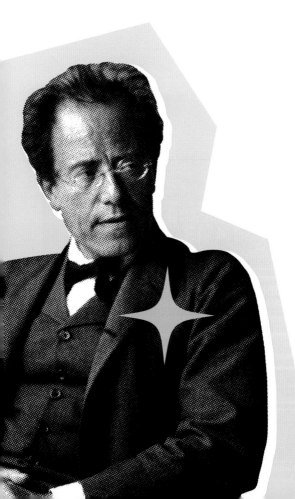

'My first work in which I found myself as "Mahler".' That was how the composer summed up his early cantata *Das klagende Lied* ('The Song of Weeping' or 'Lamentation'). He was right. During his studies at the Vienna Conservatory (1875–8) Mahler had written several substantial pieces, but what survives suggests that he was still digesting the influences of his musical heroes – Schubert, Schumann, Bruckner, Brahms. With *Das klagende Lied*, begun the year he graduated, we step into new territory – enticing, but also full of foreboding.

The first version of the work, the one performed at this year's Proms (as opposed to the more grown-up revision), shows that the power of suggestion, expressive intensity and vivid colours so typical of Mahler seem to have been there from the start. When he entered it for the Conservatory's Beethoven Prize in 1881 it was too much for the jury (which included Johannes Brahms), and they rejected it unanimously. But now we can see it as a brilliantly original evocation of the dark magic of the famous Brothers Grimm fairy tales, foundational texts for the 19th-century German Romantic movement.

The story is both lurid and deliciously exciting. In the first movement, 'Forest Legend', the elder of two brothers competing for the hand of a beautiful queen kills his younger sibling in the forest. In 'The Minstrel' a wandering minstrel discovers a bone in the forest and carves it into a flute. As he plays, the younger brother's ghostly voice speaks through the flute, telling of the forest fratricide. The third movement depicts the lavish wedding of the elder brother. The minstrel turns up and begins to play. The murderer seizes the flute, then hears his dead brother's voice exposing his crime, at which everything falls apart – literally: the queen faints, the revellers scatter in terror and the castle collapses.

It could all so easily have tipped over into absurdity, but Mahler was a master sound-painter, with a wonderful feeling for nature, and an ability to evoke the spirit of folk song without falling into fake-folksy cuteness. That delicate balance between childlike sweetness and a very adult awareness of sinister instinctual forces is evoked so tellingly that it can haunt the imagination long after the music is over. And Mahler the great musical storyteller, who can grip your attention throughout an 80-minute purely orchestral symphony, is on form right from the start. However unlikely the storyline, the music seduces and shocks us into believing in it. From the moment the minstrel picks up the bone, we know the murderer's fate is sealed. ●

Stephen Johnson is the author of books on Mahler, Bruckner, Wagner and Shostakovich, and a regular contributor to *BBC Music Magazine*. For 14 years he was a presenter of BBC Radio 3's *Discovering Music*. He now works both as a freelance writer and as a composer.

Mahler Das klagende Lied
4 AUGUST

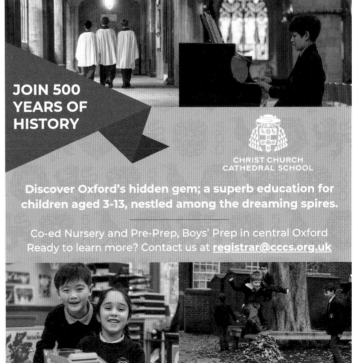

Sing Joyfully

Still only 25 years old, Samara Joy has taken the jazz world by storm with her impressive vocal ability and infectious stage presence. **JUMOKÉ FASHOLA** speaks to the singer-songwriter about her early inspirations and subsequent jazz awakening, and finds out what to expect from Joy's much-anticipated Proms debut this summer

Samara Joy's rise from her roots in the Bronx, New York, to international singing sensation is impressive. She has already earned five Grammys – her first in 2023 for *Linger Awhile*, which won Best Jazz Vocal Album as well as Best New Artist, and her latest two in February this year, including another Best Jazz Vocal Album for *A Joyful Holiday*. Despite these accomplishments, when we speak the singer is quick to reflect on the challenges and whirlwind of emotions that come with such a meteoric rise. 'It's been quite a ride,' she says. 'I'm not sure I can fully express how wonderful the journey has been. It's surreal to have won another two Grammys this year, for which I am grateful. It's been overwhelming, yet incredibly exciting.'

Her latest album, *Portrait*, features a blend of original compositions and reimagined standards. It's a rich tapestry of sounds – timeless jazz, new avant-garde creations and exuberant rhythms – that represent where she is now as an artist. 'I feel like I've grown a lot more confident in my musical vision,' she says. 'I've embraced music I thought I couldn't sing at first. I always knew I loved to sing but I never imagined I'd find this path in jazz.' After all, it was gospel that came first – and that genre still holds a profound personal connection: Joy's grandfather, now in his nineties, led a family gospel group, and

music has always been a cornerstone of their gatherings. 'Gospel is foundational to my life. Every Thanksgiving, every family gathering, we would all sing together,' she recalls. That experience shaped her musical ear, instilling a natural sense of improvisation and storytelling.

The shift towards jazz came during an audition for New York's Purchase College School of the Arts – a life-changing moment. Joy performed the only jazz song she knew. 'Thankfully they permitted me to sing a gospel song *a cappella* as a second tune,' she laughs. Encountering jazz for the first time felt akin to learning a new language. 'I wanted to feel just as confident about jazz as I did about gospel,' she explains. 'I knew I adored gospel music and could reference songs without having listened to them in detail. I wanted to have that same level of confidence and familiarity with jazz.'

Has she ever felt the pressure to go in a different direction? 'I've been pretty steadfast in what I want to present,' she says. 'I know how I felt when I first heard singers like Betty Carter and Sarah Vaughan, and musicians like Charlie Parker and Dizzy Gillespie. That was what I wanted to explore. I don't have to compromise any part of myself or any part of my message to do it … I know that everybody hears certain things in what I can do, and all the music I'm influenced by, which is incredible, but jazz is still uncharted territory for me. I don't think I will ever grow tired of it, or feel bound by any preconceived notions of what it is. It's like I'm offering my voice to the genre.

It's become a part of me, and I feel I can present that authentically to people – to be myself and not compromise.'

That ethos and inspiration extend into her self-penned music, becoming a prism through which she views everything she does as a vocalist, bandleader and songwriter. In her first original composition, 'Peace of Mind', which builds on a tune by legendary composer and bandleader Sun Ra, and which features on *Portrait*, she offers a message of hope for her fans – that 'everything will be alright, even in life's toughest moments. Your dreams will come true in ways you never imagined or expected, just as they did for me.'

> " Jazz is still uncharted territory for me. I don't think I will ever grow tired of it, or feel bound by any preconceived notions of what it is. It's like I'm offering my voice to the genre. It's become a part of me, and I feel I can present that authentically. "

This is proving to be another busy year for Joy. She tours Asia with her Octet and makes appearances at New York's Carnegie Hall and the Montreal Jazz Festival before coming to the UK this summer for her Proms debut with the BBC Concert Orchestra – an ensemble well practised at introducing debut and

Samara Joy at this year's Grammy Awards, where she picked up two wins: Best Jazz Vocal Album for *A Joyful Holiday* and Best Jazz Performance for 'Twinkle Twinkle Little Me'

non-classical artists to the festival. It will also be Joy's first time performing publicly with a full orchestra. 'At first I didn't believe that it was actually going to be at the Royal Albert Hall,' she laughs. 'Then, when I realised it would be such a big production, I started planning immediately! All the ideas began to flow. I had a whole set list drafted, and a set list of who's arranging what. I'm really excited to see it come to life.'

The concert promises to mix Joy's various influences, from blues to music by legendary pianist Thelonious Monk and vocalist Betty Carter. 'It will be a glimpse into the music that shapes my identity – and each song in the set has a purpose.' She is particularly excited to perform 'Le Sucrier Velours' from Duke Ellington's *The Queen's Suite*. Originally composed for Queen Elizabeth II after the pair met, the suite was pressed into a single vinyl copy and sent directly to the monarch as a gift. Ellington was adamant that it should not be released to the public, so it was only finally issued in 1976, two years after his death. 'That's part of what's special about that one,' explains Joy. 'It's a nice tidbit, and I figured it would be a unique song to do in London.' Other tunes on the set list include the Sinatra classic 'Day by Day' and 'You Stepped Out of a Dream', used in the 1941 movie *Ziegfeld Girl* – both of which appear on *Portrait*. We also hear Hoagy Carmichael's 'Stardust', an iconic track whose previous interpreters include John Coltrane, Ella Fitzgerald, Nat King Cole and Glenn Miller.

Joining Joy on stage will be her octet, several members of which have written orchestral arrangements especially. 'I figured that'll be fun – they already know the octet arrangements and have the charts.' Has she thought about what she might wear? 'I'm hoping to buy a whole new wardrobe when we tour Asia,' she laughs. 'I know it's gotta be two sets' worth of looks!'

Joy has become a jazz siren for Gen Z as she attracts both enthusiasts and newcomers into the fold. Her resolve to push boundaries and inspire others to do the same solidifies her role as an important figure in the contemporary jazz scene. Yet, despite the accolades and comparisons to greats such as Ella Fitzgerald and Carmen McRae, Joy remains determined not to rest on her laurels. 'I want to be open to exploring something new within myself. That's what this band and our non-stop touring have brought me.' She sees every performance as an opportunity to reach greater heights. 'I want it to be a consistent experience. I want every word that I sing to be heard very clearly. I want all of the songs to be understood. I want the energy that we're pouring out on stage to be returned back to us. And to never, never let there be a stale moment.' ●

Jumoké Fashola is a journalist, broadcaster and vocalist who currently presents a range of arts and culture programmes on BBC Radios 3 and 4 and on BBC London.

The Great American Songbook and Beyond with Samara Joy
19 JULY

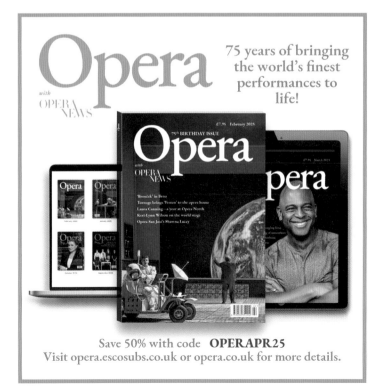
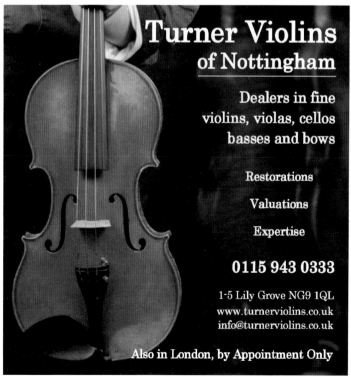

Mood Music

Ahead of the 2025 Proms season, three BBC-commissioned composers put their creative process under the microscope, arranging the themes and inspirations behind their new compositions into a series of musical 'mood boards'

Mark Simpson

ZEBRA (or, 2-3-74: The Divine Invasion of Philip K. Dick)
BBC commission: world premiere
22 JULY

ZEBRA is Mark Simpson's second Proms commission and his fourth work to be heard at the festival. It explores a series of intense hallucinations documented by sci-fi novelist Philip K. Dick in 1974. Dick claimed that a bright, pink light, originating from a woman's necklace, had uploaded mystical information into his brain. He heard cryptic messages, witnessed scenes from ancient Rome superimposed onto his neighbourhood, and saw beams of red and gold energy. The source, he believed, was a benevolent being which, because it was camouflaged from view, he nicknamed … Zebra.

A British Broadcaster
Simpson and the BBC go way back: in 2006 he won both the BBC Young Musician of the Year (as a clarinettist) and the *Guardian*/Proms Young Composers' Competition. He has been a BBC Radio 3 New Generation Artist and, from 2015 to 2019, was Composer in Residence with the BBC Philharmonic Orchestra. *ZEBRA* represents the latest step in this long and fruitful relationship.

BBC
Maida Vale
Studios
Home of the BBC Symphony Orchestra
and the Radiophonic Workshop
1934

BBC HERITAGE TRAIL

The Visionary

In the 1970s Philip K. Dick experienced a series of powerful hallucinations which he later refered to as '2-3-74' (February and March, 1974). Simpson describes *ZEBRA* as 'a musical exploration of this wonderfully weird, multitudinous and complicated spiritual experience'.

Pencil and Paper

Simpson always composes by hand – with pencil and paper – at the piano. This sketch for 'Horselover Fat's Hymn of the Soul', the second part of *ZEBRA*, offers an early peek at the work in progress.

Musical Trip

Mystical or transcendental experiences are a recurring theme in Simpson's music. He is currently writing a series of works inspired by poet Henri Michaux, who famously experimented with mescaline (NH_2). This psychedelic drug occurs naturally in some cacti.

Guitar Hero

ZEBRA is written for solo electric guitar and large orchestra – and with Scottish guitarist Sean Shibe specifically in mind. Shibe, also a former BBC Radio 3 New Generation Artist, is the soloist this summer.

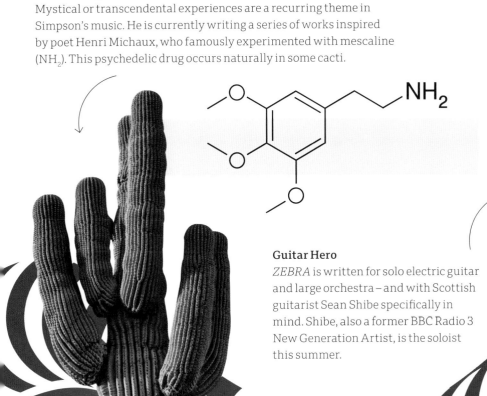

Anna Thorvaldsdottir

Before we fall (Cello Concerto)
BBC co-commission: UK premiere
13 AUGUST

Anna Thorvaldsdottir has become an increasingly influential figure in contemporary music, her vast, elemental soundscapes and 'seemingly boundless textural imagination' (*New York Times*) earning her admirers around the world. Like her 2022 Proms co-commission *ARCHORA*, the Cello Concerto *Before we fall* is not a descriptive work, nor does any of this imagery – supplied by Thorvaldsdottir herself – represent what the piece is 'about'. Instead, it reflects some of the central ideas that Thorvaldsdottir uses, while composing, 'to intuitively tap into parts of the core energy, structure, atmosphere and material of the music'. In other words, they illustrate the sparks – or 'fuel' – for her initial musical ideas, with each element containing qualities that she finds musically captivating.

Distortion
Along with deep lyricism, the Cello Concerto is characterised by a sense of distorted energy of various kinds (photo: Iceland's Reykjanes Peninsula).

Essence and Lyricism
Thorvaldsdottir says that deep lyricism lies at the heart of her Cello Concerto. She feels in touch with her own self most strongly when surrounded by nature.

Potency

Created by Thorvaldsdottir's husband, Hrafn Asgeirsson, this abstract artwork plays with 'the energy emanating from a light source'. It relates to the importance of how each note in *Before we fall* – however short – is 'fully present and sustained to its fullest duration'.

Opposing Forces

A multitude of opposites are at work in *Before we fall*, creating an 'entropic pull stabilised by lyricism and distorted energy'. This image, taken in New York City, captures the contrast between nature and edifice, and illustrates that opposition.

Terra firma

A sustained harmonic presence in *Before we fall* provides the 'earth' – what Thorvaldsdottir calls 'the grounding power of a stable foundation' – for the solo cello.

Momentum

This photograph of Thorvaldsdottir walking along a path near her home in the Surrey countryside mirrors the sense of strong forward-moving energy in *Before we fall*, which 'connects and balances opposing forces in different ways'.

Errollyn Wallen

The Elements *BBC commission: world premiere*
18 JULY

Master of the King's Music Errollyn Wallen is something of a British musical institution. She has composed music for the opening ceremony of the London 2012 Paralympic Games, Queen Elizabeth II's Golden and Diamond jubilees and, in 2020, the Last Night of the Proms. For this season's First Night she has written 'a work about the act of creation and the art of orchestration'. It explores the 'periodic table of orchestral elements' that she must work with when composing. On a deeper level, the piece is also a comment on how all instruments ultimately derive from the natural world, and how music specifically has a simple, self-evident quality that can sidestep most dogma: 'As in our world, the elemental is felt but the meaning can be elusive. While the composer advises, the listener decides.'

A Splash of Colour

For Wallen, music 'feels so closely aligned with the visual world as to be inseparable from it'. When composing, she blends tones, pitches and forces in the same way a painter uses colour, light and texture. The artist's palette, and the theory of complementary colours, provides her with a structure for fitting musical 'elements' together.

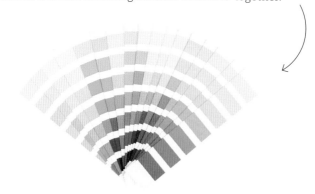

To the Lighthouse

Wallen's lighthouse home, at Strathy Point in the far north of Scotland, offers the space and silence she needs for maximum productivity: 'From there I have seen the Northern Lights. There I have complete solitude and sprawling skies.'

Music Matter

Wallen says that composition is all about manipulating the experience of time passing – about stretching and compressing it. This was particularly apparent in her 2008 choral symphony *Carbon 12*. Here, time and matter came to be represented by a lump of coal.

Grand Plans

Stravinsky once said: 'The piano is the fulcrum of all my musical discoveries. Each note that I write is tried on it, and every relationship of notes is taken apart and heard on it again and again.' Wallen, who also composes at the piano, is in full agreement.

Water Power

'Water,' says Wallen, 'is a theme often present in my work. Much of my life has been spent by the Thames in Greenwich … The movement, the colour, the texture of the water is never boring. When the storm comes I feel as if I am on a ship at sea.'

Out of the Fire

Ashes are the remembrance of fire – a nod to the burning furnaces used to forge metallic instruments, and the 'elemental' quality that each therefore posseses.

Let Her Eat Cake

'Anyone who knows anything about me knows about my deep and sustaining relationship with cake.' And Battenberg is 'the pinnacle of the cakemaker's art', offering 'a vital source of concentrated energy' while Wallen composes.

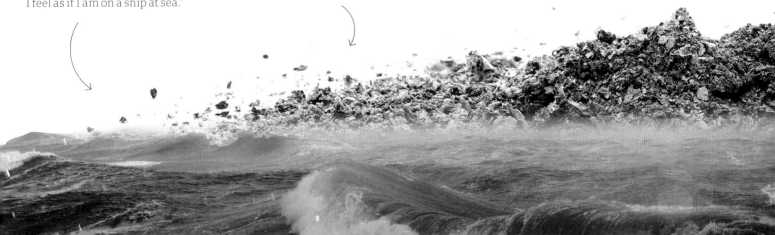

Discover ...

CAROLINE SHAW'S
The Observatory

ELIZABETH ALKER zooms in on a work inspired by a wide-angle view of the city streets below and the skies above, written by a Pulitzer Prize-winning American composer

Caroline Shaw was born in Greenville, North Carolina, in 1982 and grew up singing in her local Episcopal church choir, taking violin lessons before graduating first from Rice University and then from Yale. In 2013 her *Partita for 8 Voices*, written for Roomful of Teeth – the vocal ensemble of which she was a member – made her the youngest-ever winner of the Pulitzer Prize for Music, and it was the first piece of hers that I encountered. Like the millions of others who have streamed *Partita* online since its release in 2012, I was completely beguiled and bewildered by its strange vocal techniques – gasps, pants, whispers and low, droney hums – and the moments that gleam with very pretty and melancholy melodies. In so much of her work, Shaw employs the sparseness and emotive chord shifts of pop music. It's thanks to a lifelong love of classical music and her schooling in composition that she is able to balance this spareness with complexity, dissonance and surprise.

Shaw likes to imagine 'some kind of visual' as a guide when writing a new piece, and for *The Observatory* she visited the famous Griffith Observatory in the Hollywood Hills, taking in the view of Los Angeles sprawling out towards the distant coastline. The grid road system and the curves of the city edge contrast with the vastness of the sky and thoughts of space, which has been studied from that spot – California's so-called Gateway to the Cosmos – since the Observatory opened in 1935. In the music, we hear clear block shapes, big bold chords that move in steady sequences, bursts of brass and timpani alongside lighter dancing, swirling and concentric patterns in the woodwind and strings. The straight lines of the city meet visions of stars, moons and planets in orbit. The quotations from works including Richard Strauss's *Don Juan*, Bach's Brandenburg Concerto No. 3, Sibelius's Symphony No. 2 and Brahms's Symphony No. 1 bring suspense and drama – a narrative and textural palette that feels cinematic, as befits such a widescreen impression of space and this particular city.

Shaw bounces between broad brush-strokes of orchestral colour, quieter solo piano passages and delicate twinkling percussive sections; and between references to those epic classical works and moments that soar like the title-sequence to a sci-fi blockbuster. As she explains, there is 'chaos and clarity': all that we know and yet fail to understand about the glittering uninhabited expanse above us and the vibrancy of life below. Shaw's referencing of works from the classical canon within a contemporary piece is a nod to the eternal quest of human beings to see and understand the universe and our place within it. ●

Elizabeth Alker presents *Classical Live*, *Unclassified* and the words and music programme *Northern Drift* for Radio 3. She co-curates the *Unclassified Live* concert series and has produced documentaries for Radio 4, Radio 2 and Radio 1. Her book *Everything We Do Is Music* is due to be published in August (Faber).

Caroline Shaw The Observatory
9 AUGUST

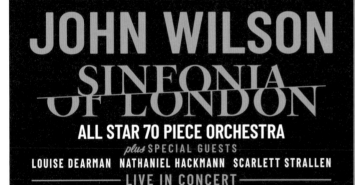

SHOCK AND AWE

Bernard Herrmann scored eight of Alfred Hitchcock's films but could equally turn his hand to sci-fi, adventure and opera. Fifty years after his death, **JULIE HUBBERT** outlines a career that ranged from *Citizen Kane* to *Taxi Driver*

It's the 1950s. The world has just wrapped up its second great war. England is exhausted and America is disillusioned. Hollywood is retreating into big-budget biblical epics and moral crusades, and American cinema is hung-over with post-war stress: on screen, John Wayne crumbles, Frank Sinatra shoots heroin, Vivien Leigh goes insane and Susan Hayward is executed for murder.

Enter Alfred Hitchcock and Bernard Herrmann, id and ego to a new kind of American psychodrama. British film-maker Hitchcock was drawn to Hollywood money and Herrmann, an American composer and conductor, was drawn to film. They made eight pictures between 1955 and 1964 that redefined American cinema as a bubbling cauldron of neuroses, psychoses, conspiracy and violence. Hitchcock's progressive style offered introspective images and minimal dialogue, and substituted verbal exposition with Herrmann's inventive music. Their collaboration was dark and magical, producing classics we continue to cherish today.

Herrmann perfected a sparse, ambiguous language for their first three thrillers – *The Trouble with Harry* (1955), *The Man Who Knew too Much* (1956) and *The Wrong Man* (also 1956) – but the composer quickly stepped beyond his own formula. In

◄ Spiralling emotions: poster for Hitchcock's *Vertigo*, in whose score Bernard Herrmann captured the growing obsession of detective Scottie Ferguson (James Stewart) with his subject, Madeleine Elster (Kim Novak)

North By Northwest (1959) he serenaded a bachelor entangled with international criminals with an offbeat Cuban habanera. In *Vertigo* (1958) he wrote a score as lush as a Wagner opera. And who can forget the infamous score of *Psycho* (1960), in which 24 shrieking string instruments articulate the screams of a psychopath's victims? By the time we reach *The Birds* in 1963, Herrmann doesn't write a single note – he simply generates eerie bird sounds.

The Hitchcock thriller, however, isn't the only arena in which Herrmann made his mark. He also composed for the period's best sci-fi movies. In *The Day the Earth Stood Still* (1951) he invoked spooky alien terror by use of the theremin, the eerily swooping early electronic instrument that became a favourite of composers for the genre. *Beneath the 12-Mile Reef* (1953) features the exuberant glissandos of a dozen harps, while in *Journey to the Center of the Earth* (1959) the obsolete 16th-century serpent (formerly the bass instrument of the cornett family) conveys the planet's molten interior. When adventure escapades were subject to the special-effects wizardry of Ray Harryhausen in *The 7th Voyage of Sinbad* (1958), *Mysterious Island* (1961) and *Jason and the Argonauts* (1963), Herrmann jumped into the creative fray with his best experimental scoring. He also composed for popular TV shows such as *The Twilight Zone*, *Gunsmoke* and *Have Gun – Will Travel*.

Herrmann started out as a conductor in 1934, with the CBS Symphony Orchestra in New York. When CBS expanded into radio dramas, he was hired to compose

music cues, and when the network added theatrical sensation Orson Welles to its stable of talent, Herrmann became an indispensable member of the crew for Welles's radio drama series *The Mercury Theater on the Air*.

After this, Hollywood came calling for Welles, but he refused to make movies without Herrmann. Their first picture together, *Citizen Kane* (1941), is a masterpiece of cinematic art. They made two additional films, *The Magnificent Ambersons* (1942) and *Jane Eyre* (1943), before a nasty dispute with studio executives prompted Welles to flee Hollywood for Europe.

Throughout the 1940s Herrmann continued on-air to conduct the CBS Symphony Orchestra with distinction, programming new American and British composers, in contrast to the old European music that Toscanini served up at rival station NBC. He was a champion and friend of the great Charles Ives. He also wrote his own concert music – an orchestral homage to the Christmas card lithographers in the *Currier and Ives Suite* (1935), vocal cantatas based on *Moby-Dick* (1937) and *Johnny Appleseed* (1940), and a neo-Romantic Symphony No. 1 (1941), all demonstrating his enduring inspiration from literary sources. The Anglophilia that fuelled the score for *The Ghost and Mrs. Muir* (1947) compelled him to write an opera, *Wuthering Heights*, completed in 1951.

Herrmann's iconic collaboration with Hitchcock and his Hollywood career came to an end in 1966, due partly to a similarity of personalities: Herrmann's abrasiveness was legendary, but both men were intransigent to the point of stubbornness. Musical tastes were also changing and the studios wanted movies with popular theme songs that they could sell to younger viewers. When executives demanded that Hitchcock's *Torn Curtain* (1966) have a theme song, Hitchcock agreed but Herrmann refused to subject his talent to the commercial interests of the studio, bringing his relationship with Hitchcock and Hollywood to an abrupt close.

The composer moved to London, where he produced two inspired scores for French New Wave director François Truffaut – *Fahrenheit 451* (1966) and *The Bride Wore Black* (1968). Brian De Palma rediscovered Herrmann for his Hitchcockian homage, *Sisters* (1972), and the young auteur Martin Scorsese hired him to write a jazz score for his neo-noir drama *Taxi Driver* (1976).

When Herrmann passed away the day after recording the *Taxi Driver* score, his obituaries shone with praise for his uncompromising talent. They marked him, as we should today, as a true American maverick in an age of anxiety. ●

Julie Hubbert is the LaDare Robinson Memorial Professor of Music and Professor of Film and Media Studies at the University of South Carolina. She is the editor of *Celluloid Symphonies: Texts and Contexts in Film Music History* (Univ. of California Press, 2011) and author of the forthcoming book *Technology, Listening, and Labor: Music in New Hollywood Film (1967–1980)* (OUP).

Classic Thriller Soundtracks

4 SEPTEMBER

Murder at the RAH

The Royal Albert Hall takes centre-stage in Hitchcock and Herrmann's second collaboration

Benjamin McKenna (James Stewart) peers down from a box in the Royal Albert Hall to see the assassin sprawled below in Hitchcock's *The Man Who Knew too Much* (1956)

There are some curious things about *The Man Who Knew too Much*, the second film Herrmann made with Alfred Hitchcock. For starters, it's a remake of a movie Hitchcock had already shot in 1934 for Gaumont-British studios. It's not often a director gets a second go at the same film but Hitchcock was fond of its unusual plot and, by 1956, wanted to remake the movie in Technicolor, with a bigger 'Hollywood' budget. A new screenwriter updated the characters, relocated the opening action to exotic Morocco, and the story of the McKenna family's brush with international intrigue and assassination unfolded, this time with Americans in the lead roles.

Part of Hitchcock's interest in remaking the film was the chance to stage its novel assassination scene at a concert at the Royal Albert Hall. For budget and technical reasons, the original had been shot on a sound stage outside London, but this time the performers and concert hall were real. Hitchcock also relished the idea of expanding the film's key scene, where the assassin must release his bullet during the final cymbal crash of a large choral cantata. It's an unusual plot device centred on musical literacy, and one can see why Hitchcock would have enjoyed perfecting it.

He also wanted to retain the music from the original film but needed the scene to be longer. Curiously, Herrmann agreed to reuse the *Storm Cloud Cantata* – a choral work written for the 1934 original by Australian composer Arthur Benjamin – and he added several minutes to the orchestral opening. The result is an action-packed montage that spans 12 minutes without a single word of dialogue. D. B. Wyndham Lewis's original text was largely preserved, with its imagery of dying moons and screaming birds, and the storm remained a metaphor for murder. Herrmann's reorchestration added brilliance to the fanfares, lush harps to the lyrical interludes and the Hall's powerful pipe organ to the climax. Herrmann performed the cantata on screen himself, marking not just his debut as a film actor, but also as a conductor, both of the London Symphony Orchestra and at the Royal Albert Hall – achievements he sought in real life. Hitchcock cheekily captured this irony in a shot of the posterboards outside the Hall advertising the fake performance.

Hitchcock's fondness for blond actresses and good popular music led him to cast singer Doris Day as his female lead. Paramount executives could not pass up the opportunity to extract a hit song from the project and demanded that Day both sing in the film and record a song. Hitchcock dutifully worked the enigmatic 'Que sera, sera' by Evans and Livingston into the film. The song won the title's only Oscar. When Herrmann heard it, he characteristically muttered, 'Why do you want a piece of junk like that in the picture?' He hadn't written it, after all!

Julie Hubbert

BBC RADIO 3

ADVENTURES
IN CLASSICAL

Listen on SOUNDS

MERCHANT TAYLORS'
School

Handmade,
for you.

Merchant Taylors' is renowned for its outstanding academic education. Our mission is to truly know each pupil. We support them in exploring world-class opportunities, helping them discover and develop their unique talents.

Book your visit now

to meet our passionate music faculty and learn more about scholarships.

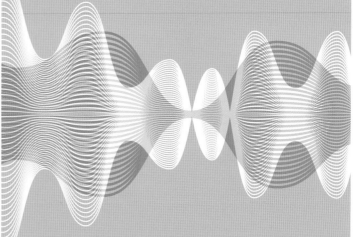

Philharmonia

We're celebrating our 80th birthday and we've invited...

Santtu-Matias Rouvali **Marin Alsop** Víkingur Ólafsson **Gabriela Ortiz**
Evgeny Kissin **Lorenzo Viotti** Jakub Hrůša **Denis Kozhukhin** Hilary Hahn
Masabane Cecilia Rangwanasha **Frank Dupree** Bruce Liu **Kent Nagano**
Fazil Say Pacho Flores Sean Shibe **Christian Lindberg** Alisa Weilerstein
Benjamin Grosvenor **Esa-Pekka Salonen** Lisa Batiashvili **Nicola Benedetti**

You're invited too!
Book now for our 2025/26 season at the Royal Festival Hall

Tickets from £10
philharmonia.co.uk
0800 652 6717

**SOUTHBANK
CENTRE**
RESIDENT

Supported using public funding by
**ARTS COUNCIL
ENGLAND**

The Proms on TV

On behalf of all of us at BBC Television, I am delighted to be bringing some of the world's greatest musicians to your screens as part of this year's Proms. Last year we reached a record 12.5 million viewers, and this year's line-up promises to be just as compelling, with a vibrant range of concerts from the Royal Albert Hall as well as the first televised Prom outside of London, from Gateshead's Glasshouse International Centre for Music.

Whether you are a long-time classical music fan or watching for the first time, there is something for everyone to enjoy this season. Highlights on TV include Nicholas McCarthy's Proms debut with Ravel's Piano Concerto for the Left Hand, Sir Simon Rattle conducting the Chineke! Orchestra and the Aurora Orchestra performing Shostakovich by heart. Anoushka Shankar also makes a return to the Proms, while the National Youth Orchestra performs *The Planets* and music from *Star Wars*; and, of course, there will be all the usual favourites on BBC One as part of the Last Night.

Finally, we welcome *The Traitors* to this year's Proms as Claudia Winkleman introduces music from and inspired by the hit BBC series. So, to the Proms Faithful and new recruits alike, here's to another year of passion and inspiration.

Suzy Klein
Head of Arts and Classical Music TV

Date	Programme	Channel
18 July	First Night of the Proms 2025	live on **TWO**
19 July	The Great American Songbook and Beyond with Samara Joy	**FOUR**
20 July	Vivaldi and Bach	**FOUR**
20 July	Ravel's Piano Concerto for the Left Hand	**FOUR**
25 July	Beethoven's Fifth	**TWO**
26 July	Bach and Mendelssohn with the Royal Northern Sinfonia	**FOUR**
26 July	The Traitors	**BBC**
2 Aug	Viennese Whirl	**TWO**
3 Aug	Soul Revolution	**TWO**
5 Aug	Great British Classics	**TWO**
7 Aug	Dvořák's 'New World' Symphony	**FOUR**
9 Aug	The Planets and Star Wars	**TWO**
12 Aug	Anoushka Shankar: 'Chapters'	**FOUR**
16 Aug	Shostakovich's Fifth by Heart	**FOUR**
21 Aug	Beethoven's Ninth	**FOUR**
23 Aug	Mäkelä Conducts Mahler's Fifth	**FOUR**
25 Aug	CBeebies Prom: A Magical Bedtime Story	**CBeebies**
4 Sep	Classic Thriller Soundtracks	**FOUR**
5 Sep	Rattle Conducts Chineke!	**FOUR**
9 Sep	Vienna Philharmonic Plays Mozart and Tchaikovsky	**FOUR**
13 Sep	Last Night of the Proms 2025	first half live on **TWO** second half live on **ONE**

Please visit bbc.co.uk/proms for the latest broadcast information

Concert Listings

Full details of all the 2025 BBC Proms concerts – 72 Proms at the Royal Albert Hall, plus residencies in Gateshead and Bristol and concerts in Belfast, Bradford and Sunderland – are listed in these pages, alongside Spotlight interviews with 25 artists.

For an at-a-glance calendar of the whole season, see inside back cover.

Please check the BBC Proms website for the latest information: bbc.co.uk/proms.

We hope you enjoy a summer of world-class music-making.

PROGRAMME CHANGES
Concert details were correct at the time of going to press. The BBC reserves the right to alter artists or programmes as necessary.

Your Summer at the Proms

Book your tickets

Book seated tickets online, in person or by phone from Saturday 17 May. £8 standing tickets are available online on the day. Or, save money by buying Promming Season Passes. *See pages 147–149 for details.*

Enjoy the concert

These performances are available to everyone, whether you're attending in person, listening live on Radio 3 or BBC Sounds or watching on BBC TV or iPlayer.

Relive the experience

You can catch up with every Prom on BBC Sounds and all televised Proms on BBC iPlayer.

Friday 18 July

7pm–c9.20pm • Royal Albert Hall

● £26–£86 *(plus booking fee*)*

LISA BATIASHVILI

First Night of the Proms 2025

Bliss Birthday Fanfare for Sir Henry Wood 2'

Mendelssohn Overture 'The Hebrides' ('Fingal's Cave') 10'

Sibelius Violin Concerto in D minor 35'

INTERVAL

Errollyn Wallen The Elements c10'
BBC commission: world premiere

Vaughan Williams Sancta civitas 30'

Lisa Batiashvili *violin*
Caspar Singh *tenor*
Gerald Finley *bass-baritone*

BBC Singers
BBC Symphony Chorus
Members of London Youth Choirs
BBC Symphony Orchestra
Sakari Oramo *conductor*

The crash of the seas, the crumbling of city walls and a glimpse of the heavens: welcome to the 2025 First Night. There's a Scottish sound-picture from Mendelssohn and cool Nordic grandeur from Sibelius. Errollyn Wallen harnesses primal forces in her new orchestral commission, while visions from the Book of Revelation are the starting point for Vaughan Williams's *Sancta civitas. See pages 96–97.*

🖥 *Broadcast live on BBC Two and BBC iPlayer*

Saturday 19 July

7pm–c9.30pm • Royal Albert Hall

● £11–£56 *(plus booking fee*)*

SAMARA JOY

The Great American Songbook and Beyond with Samara Joy

Samara Joy

Samara Joy Octet
BBC Concert Orchestra
Miho Hazama *conductor*

There will be one interval

A No. 1 album and a double Grammy-win in 2023 put Samara Joy on the map, establishing the young American artist as 'the next jazz sensation' and 'a legend in the making', regularly compared to Ella Fitzgerald and Sarah Vaughan. Fresh from another double win at this year's Grammys, Joy makes a much-anticipated Proms debut, introducing audiences to her electric combination of youthful energy and old-soul musical style. The evening features classic songs and unique twists on instrumental standards, from bossa nova to the Great American Songbook. Along the way she salutes figures including Vaughan, Fitzgerald, Duke Ellington and Billie Holiday. *See pages 88–90.*

🖥 *Broadcast on BBC Four and BBC iPlayer this season*

Sunday 20 July

11am–c1pm • Royal Albert Hall ☀

● £11–£56 *(plus booking fee')*

THÉOTIME LANGLOIS DE SWARTE

Vivaldi and Bach

Programme to include:

Vivaldi
Violin Concerto in A minor, RV 356   7'
Violin Concerto in D minor, RV 813   9'
Trio Sonata in D minor, 'La follia'   10'
Concerto for strings in G minor,
RV 157   6'
The Four Seasons – 'Summer'   10'

J. S. Bach
Orchestral Suite No. 3 in D major,
BWV 1068 – Air   4'
Violin Concerto in G minor,
BWV 1056R – Largo   4'

and works by Avison, Marcello and Matteis Jr

Le Consort
Théotime Langlois de Swarte *violin/director*

There will be one interval

Still in his twenties, French violinist Théotime Langlois de Swarte combines supple athleticism with precocious musical intelligence. He makes a much-anticipated Proms debut as soloist with his ensemble Le Consort, in a programme built around violin concertos by Vivaldi and the repertoire that first lit the touchpaper for the talented young musician as a teenager.

🖵 *Broadcast on BBC Four and BBC iPlayer this season*

Sunday 20 July

7.30pm–c9.45pm • Royal Albert Hall

● £11–£56 *(plus booking fee')*

NICHOLAS McCARTHY

Ravel's Piano Concerto for the Left Hand

Shostakovich, arr. Atovmyan
Suite for Variety Orchestra   22'
Ravel
Piano Concerto for the Left Hand   19'

INTERVAL

Walton Symphony No. 1
in B flat minor   43'

Nicholas McCarthy *piano*

Bournemouth Symphony Orchestra
Mark Wigglesworth *conductor*

All swagger, originality and 'orgiastic power', one of the great 20th-century symphonies, Walton's First put the composer on the map – as the heir to both Elgar and Sibelius. Ravel's jazz-infused, darkly atmospheric Piano Concerto for the Left Hand also breaks new ground: only one hand plays, though the ear hears all the richness of two. Nicholas McCarthy – the world's only professional one-handed concert pianist – makes his Proms debut. The Bournemouth Symphony Orchestra opens its first Prom under new Chief Conductor Mark Wigglesworth with Shostakovich's jovial *Suite for Variety Orchestra*, packed with tunes from the composer's music for ballet, theatre and cinema. *See pages 22–26, 58–62.*

🖵 *Broadcast on BBC Four and BBC iPlayer this season*

Spotlight on ...
Mark Wigglesworth • 20 July

'I think an ideal concert programme has as many contrasts as it does connections.' Mark Wigglesworth is pondering the trio of works for which he conducts the Bournemouth Symphony Orchestra on 20 July. Indeed, for many, Ravel's Piano Concerto for the Left Hand and Walton's First Symphony sound poles apart, technically and emotionally. 'What I love about the Ravel,' he continues, 'is that there's no concession to the fact that the pianist is playing with one hand. The music makes a point of using both extremes of the piano's register. There's not a second where you feel anything is missing.' Walton's symphony, however, 'transcends its English roots to sound genuinely universal in its description of the human condition,' he feels. 'It's not so much a journey from darkness to light as from uncertainty to confidence. The blaze of humanity that ends the work is unforgettably inspiring.'

The Prom comes at the end of Wigglesworth's first season as the BSO's Chief Conductor, though he had been Principal Guest for the previous three years. 'I love how well the musicians listen to each other, but never at the expense of self-expression – a combination that's not as easy as it sounds. It's a way of playing that needs ego and humility in equal measure, and above all an appreciation that together we can express so much more than we can on our own.'

Spotlight on ...
Anja Bihlmaier • 22 July

'From my very first concert with the BBC Philharmonic Orchestra, I felt an immediate connection.' Still partway through her debut season as Principal Guest Conductor, Anja Bihlmaier is reflecting on her relationship with the orchestra's musicians. 'They're dedicated, virtuosic and always open to new ideas – which makes every rehearsal and performance a joy. Their sense of humour also creates a wonderful working atmosphere!'

That's just as well, because it's a collection of bold, ambitious pieces that orchestra and conductor bring to their Prom on 22 July, launching with Strauss's *Death and Transfiguration*, in Bihlmaier's words nothing less than 'a journey of life, death and the transcendence of the soul'. Meanwhile the final work in Bihlmaier's Prom, Berlioz's *Symphonie fantastique,* 'plunges us into a world of obsession, ecstasy and the supernatural,' she says. 'It's one of the most extraordinary pieces in the repertoire, and I absolutely love conducting it! It tells a vivid, dramatic story – full of love, longing, obsession and nightmares – and I think it's essential to bring out its theatricality. "The Witches' Sabbath" is a nightmarish spectacle – a macabre court of the damned where souls face judgement. The atmosphere is grotesque and chilling – it sends shivers down the spine. At the Proms, with its electrifying energy, this movement will come alive in all its spine-tingling horror.'

Monday 21 July
7.30pm–*c*9.45pm • Royal Albert Hall

● £11–£56 *(plus booking fee')*

ALLAN CLAYTON

Mahler's Seventh

Tom Coult Monologues for the Curious   *c24'*
BBC commission: world premiere

INTERVAL

Mahler Symphony No. 7   *77'*

Allan Clayton tenor

BBC Philharmonic Orchestra
John Storgårds conductor

Night-time darkness and blazing musical sunlight collide in Mahler's Symphony No. 7 – a musical epic that packs the whole world into five contrasting movements. Vast orchestral forces – including mandolin, cowbells and guitar – conjure a shifting landscape of waltzes, serenades, fanfares, marches and mysterious 'night-wandering' – by turns romantic and humorous, sardonic and sincere. To open, John Storgårds conducts the BBC Philharmonic Orchestra and tenor Allan Clayton in the world premiere of award-winning composer Tom Coult's *Monologues for the Curious*, inspired by the ghost stories of M. R. James.

Tuesday 22 July
7.30pm–*c*9.50pm • Royal Albert Hall

● £11–£56 *(plus booking fee')*

SEAN SHIBE

Berlioz's 'Symphonie fantastique'

R. Strauss Death and Transfiguration   *23'*
Mark Simpson ZEBRA (or, 2-3-74: The Divine Invasion of Philip K. Dick)   *c20'*
BBC commission: world premiere

INTERVAL

Berlioz Symphonie fantastique   *49'*

Sean Shibe electric guitar

BBC Philharmonic Orchestra
Anja Bihlmaier conductor

A concert of larger-than-life sounds, stories and characters has Berlioz's *Symphonie fantastique* at its heart. Heady, opium-fuelled visions create a kaleidoscopic sequence: a swirling ballroom, a march to the scaffold and a witches' sabbath, all set to the obsessive pulse of unrequited love. Sci-fi legend Philip K. Dick inspires Mark Simpson's *ZEBRA*, a new concerto for maverick guitarist and former BBC Radio 3 New Generation Artist Sean Shibe. The concert opens with Strauss's *Death and Transfiguration* – no less than a musical struggle between life and death, climaxing in a promise of eternal peace. *See pages 92–93.*

Wednesday 23 July

6.30pm–c8.35pm • Royal Albert Hall

⬤ £11–£56 *(plus booking fee')*

CRISTIAN MĂCELARU

French Night with the Orchestre National de France

Ravel Rapsodie espagnole	16'
Joseph Bologne, Chevalier de Saint-Georges Violin Concerto in G major, Op. 8	22'

INTERVAL

Sohy Danse mystique *UK premiere*	13'
Chausson Poème	17'
Ravel La valse	12'

Randall Goosby *violin*

Orchestre National de France
Cristian Măcelaru *conductor*

Praised by the *The New York Times* for his 'exquisite tone and virtuosity', American violinist Randall Goosby makes his Proms debut in pioneering 18th-century composer Joseph Bologne's graceful Violin Concerto in G major, Op. 8, and Chausson's *Poème*, a passionate musical love letter. Cristian Măcelaru conducts the Orchestre National de France in a French-themed programme that includes two orchestral masterpieces by Ravel – the colourful *Rapsodie espagnole* and the haunting ghost-waltz *La valse* – as well as Charlotte Sohy's rhapsodic *Danse mystique. See pages 22–26, 32.*

Wednesday 23 July

10.15pm–c11.30pm • Royal Albert Hall 🌙

⬤ £11–£37 *(plus booking fee')*

Late Night

SARAH ARISTIDOU

Boulez and Berio: 20th-Century Giants

Berio Sequenza V	6'
Boulez Dialogue de l'ombre double	18'
Berio Recital I (for Cathy)	35'

Sarah Aristidou *soprano*
Jérôme Comte *clarinet*
Lucas Ounissi *trombone*
IRCAM *live electronics*

Ensemble intercontemporain
Pierre Bleuse *conductor*

There will be no interval

This season we celebrate the careers of 20th-century game-changers Pierre Boulez and Luciano Berio, whose inventive, iconoclastic legacies continue to echo through the sounds, styles and techniques of today. The Ensemble intercontemporain – founded by Boulez in 1976 – and Pierre Bleuse celebrate the pair in a concert full of sonic theatre. Boulez's tour de force for clarinet, the shadow-duet *Dialogue de l'ombre double*, meets Berio's allusive, tragicomic music-drama *Recital I*, which remixes opera's history via the composer's own distinctive imagination. Tragicomedy also streaks through Berio's *Sequenza V*, which prompts a solo trombonist to explore a plethora of unlikely playing (and vocal) techniques. *See pages 68–71.*

Spotlight on ...

Randall Goosby • 23 July

'He wasn't just an accomplished violinist, composer and conductor, he was also a champion fencer, dancer, even an army general later in his life – and people were astounded that all this talent and passion could exist in a person of colour.' Randall Goosby is talking about Joseph Bologne, whose Violin Concerto in G major, Op. 8, he performs at his Proms debut on 23 July. 'People hear his music and think it's similar to Mozart or Haydn, but really he goes so much further, with incredibly virtuosic gestures and figures that crawl all over the fingerboard. His music is so full of life, vigour, energy and movement, along with moments of incredible intimacy and tenderness.' Goosby has long championed lesser-known Black composers, seeing greater diversity as crucial to widening music's reach. 'There's been so much discussion about classical music appealing to a broader public. But there are also so many stories and lives and experiences that exist in classical music that people are completely unaware of.'

His other work in the same concert is Chausson's *Poème*. 'It's been close to my heart for a long time, but it was only after several years of playing it that I realised it was inspired by a story by Ivan Turgenev about a mystical love triangle, which completely changed my perception of the music. All of Chausson's athletics in the solo violin part make a lot more sense when you understand how magical the story is.'

Spotlight on ...
Augustin Hadelich • 24 July

Augustin Hadelich has a long history with Mendelssohn's Violin Concerto. 'I started playing it when I was 8!' he laughs. 'I never really put it away entirely, although when I was about 24 I took a step back and kind of relearnt it from scratch – a sort of reset, discarding old habits. I tried to play as if I'd never heard the piece before.' That's not easy, of course, with one of the best-loved works in the violin repertoire. If an 8-year-old can learn it, does that mean it's easy? 'It's very well written for the instrument,' Hadelich confirms, 'and it exhibits the violin's capabilities to full effect, so it's sometimes considered a good showpiece for students. But the musical challenges are significant. It might not be too difficult to play the notes, but Mendelssohn's music is so transparent, so it needs to be played with precision and lightness, and to be full of character.' That character he describes as 'extroverted, virtuosic, even flashy: the piece is so exhilarating and beautiful, it's no surprise it's such an audience favourite'.

Hadelich joins old friends Sakari Oramo and the BBC Symphony Orchestra for the Prom. 'We last worked together in 2019, with Ligeti's Violin Concerto – so this repertoire couldn't be more different! But in a life in which I travel to a different city every week, the friendships that I strike up with musicians are very special. Perhaps because Sakari is a violinist himself, I've always felt an immediate connection.'

Thursday 24 July
7.30pm–c9.35pm • Royal Albert Hall

● £11–£56 *(plus booking fee')*

SAKARI ORAMO

Mendelssohn's Violin Concerto

Stravinsky The Song of the Nightingale   21'

Mendelssohn Violin Concerto in E minor   26'

INTERVAL

Anthony Davis Tales (Tails) of the Signifying Monkey   15'
UK premiere

R. Strauss Till Eulenspiegel's Merry Pranks   15'

Augustin Hadelich *violin*

BBC Symphony Orchestra
Sakari Oramo *conductor*

Mischievous tricksters and magical fairy tales meet in a fantastical programme from Sakari Oramo and the BBC Symphony Orchestra. Incorrigible troublemaker Till Eulenspiegel is up to no good in the witty, light-footed antics of Strauss's tone-poem. A clever monkey faces off against a lion in the UK premiere of American composer Anthony Davis's *Tales (Tails) of the Signifying Monkey* and a nightingale must charm Death to spare the Emperor of China in Stravinsky's *The Song of the Nightingale*. At the heart of the programme is one of the great Romantic violin concertos: Augustin Hadelich is the soloist in Mendelssohn's vivacious, melody-filled masterpiece.

Friday 25 July
6.30pm–c9pm • Royal Albert Hall

● £11–£56 *(plus booking fee')*

ALEXANDRE KANTOROW

Beethoven's Fifth

Rameau Les Indes galantes – suite   24'

Saint-Saëns Piano Concerto No. 5 in F major, 'Egyptian'   29'

INTERVAL

Jay Capperauld Bruckner's Skull   16'

Beethoven Symphony No. 5 in C major   31'

Alexandre Kantorow *piano*

Scottish Chamber Orchestra
Maxim Emelyanychev *conductor*

The lure of the East runs through this Prom given by Maxim Emelyanychev and the Scottish Chamber Orchestra. French pianist and star of the Paris 2024 Olympics opening ceremony, Alexandre Kantorow is the soloist in Saint-Saëns's 'Egyptian' Piano Concerto – a vivid musical travelogue, lively with chirping crickets and croaking frogs – while a selection from Rameau's opera-ballet *Les Indes galantes* offers sonic snapshots from Peru, Turkey, Persia and America. Fate knocks loudly at the door in Beethoven's Fifth Symphony, answered with defiant musical optimism, but it's Death who gets the final word in Jay Capperauld's *Bruckner's Skull*.

🖥 *Broadcast on BBC Two and BBC iPlayer this season*

Saturday 26 July

3pm–c5pm & 7.30pm–c9.30pm
Royal Albert Hall

● £33–£110 *(plus booking fee*)*

The Traitors

Claudia Winkleman *presenter*

BBC Singers
BBC Scottish Symphony Orchestra
Karen Ní Bhroin *conductor*

There will be one interval

AD *Audio-described by Timna Fibert*
BSL *British Sign Language-interpreted*

By order of the Traitors, you're invited to a spine-tingling celebration of musical treachery! Claudia Winkleman is our host as we explore this worldwide television phenomenon, with its tense and haunting sound-world. From epic classical orchestral favourites to opera excerpts with betrayal at their heart, this unique Prom also features melodramatic chart tracks heard on *The Traitors* – with a gothic, symphonic twist.

Conjuring the misty intrigue worthy of a Highlands castle are the BBC Scottish Symphony Orchestra and BBC Singers, as well as special-guest soloists. There's a new take on that famous theme tune, a selection of music from the show and some familiar figures and faces from the challenges and Round Tables. A musical invitation into the world of *The Traitors* for all fans – whether you're a Faithful or a Traitor. Don a cloak, fingerless gloves and eyeliner to lose yourself in a concert like no other.

🖥 *Broadcast on BBC TV and BBC iPlayer this season*

Sunday 27 July

7.30pm–c10pm • Royal Albert Hall

● £10–£46 *(plus booking fee*)*

Mozart and Bruckner

Ryan Wigglesworth for Laura, after Bach   *c10'*
BBC commission: world premiere

Mozart Piano Concerto No. 20 in D minor   *30'*

INTERVAL

Bruckner Symphony No. 7 in E major   *64'*

Mariam Batsashvili *piano*

BBC Scottish Symphony Orchestra
Ryan Wigglesworth *conductor*

A melody heard in a dream, a tribute to a dying genius, a vision of cosmic beauty: Bruckner's Symphony No. 7 is the composer's musical memorial to Richard Wagner. It's a homage that elevated the Austrian composer to new heights, a musical walk around a magnificent cathedral. A contemporary tribute opens tonight's Prom: Ryan Wigglesworth's *for Laura, after Bach*, dedicated to the memory of former BBC Scottish Symphony Orchestra Leader Laura Samuel and inspired by her recording of a Bach Partita, played at her funeral. Mozart's stormy Piano Concerto No. 20 completes the programme, with Georgian pianist and former BBC Radio 3 New Generation Artist Mariam Batsashvili as the soloist.

Spotlight on ...
Claudia Winkleman • 26 July

Lies, subterfuge and betrayal: all the dark drama from the infamous Scottish castle spills over into the Royal Albert Hall for the first ever *Traitors* Prom. And what better match for the TV show's intrigue than tales of deception, jealousy and vengeance from the heart of classical music? The concert's mistress of ceremonies is, of course, *Traitors* host Claudia Winkleman – a Proms admirer herself. 'I've been twice and thought it was completely fantastic. The atmosphere is like nothing else.' As presenter of BBC Radio 2's *Arts Show* for almost a decade, she has broad musical interests – even if she's modest about them. 'My dad is always playing classical music, so I love it. My own music taste is pretty chronic – I like a rock band and a guitar. Stones, Oasis, Primal Scream. Anything that makes me sit up.'

Music, of course, is a crucial element in *The Traitors*' brooding atmosphere – from Sam Watts's gripping main theme to orchestral reimaginings of pop tracks. Reconceiving a TV show as a live event is quite a challenge, though – not least in bringing Winkleman up close to devoted fans of the show. How does she feel about that? 'I absolutely can't wait. One of the greatest things about being part of *The Traitors* is how people feel about it. It's a privilege to host the show and I feel the same way about being in the iconic Royal Albert Hall listening to the live music. I've asked for a cloak and an owl. I think only part of this will be successful …'

Spotlight on ...
Arooj Aftab • 29 July

Born in Lahore and now based in Brooklyn, Arooj Aftab takes an avowedly global perspective on the music she creates, blending jazz, South Asian classical, blues and folk into a style that's distinctively her own. 'The Earth is so old, and music has been moving across it for so long now that I believe all of it is intrinsically linked,' she explains. 'It's my greatest joy and what excites me the most in my own creative music process – this thing of crossover and a lot of different styles having a subtle, honest and natural-sounding kinship.'

For her Proms debut she brings together regular band members and special guests to sample tracks from her four-album back catalogue – including last year's opulent, brooding *Night Reign*: 'It will be dynamic, alive, edgy, night-prowl-oriented,' Aftab confirms. She also gets an especially lavish backing band in the form of the BBC Symphony Orchestra, conducted by Jules Buckley. 'I'm still new to the classical world,' Aftab explains. 'I come from a freer jazz background but I do appreciate the power of large orchestral arrangements and the energy they can bring to a piece.' Aftab and Buckley have worked together before with the Metropole Orkest. 'I love Jules's aesthetic,' Aftab smiles. 'It's a good and welcome challenge to work together in this way. All of us involved have to find a balance, lean into our strong areas and loosen our grip on others so it can all come together and get us to our vision.'

Monday 28 July
7.30pm–*c*9.30pm • Royal Albert Hall

● £10–£46 *(plus booking fee')*

RYAN WIGGLESWORTH

Beethoven and Birtwistle

Birtwistle Earth Dances   38'

INTERVAL

Beethoven Symphony No. 3
in E flat major, 'Eroica'   47'

BBC Scottish Symphony Orchestra
Ryan Wigglesworth *conductor*

Harrison Birtwistle's monumental *Earth Dances* returns to the Proms for the first time this century. This contemporary orchestral masterpiece boasts tectonic shifts that surge and fissure with inexorable, elemental force. Ryan Wigglesworth and the BBC Scottish Symphony Orchestra pair it with the mould-breaking orchestral pinnacle of another age. Grander than anything that came before, Beethoven's Symphony No. 3, the 'Eroica', ushers in Romanticism, revolutionising both the form itself and expectations of what a symphony can – and should – be.

Every Prom is broadcast on BBC Radio 3 and BBC Sounds

Tuesday 29 July
7.30pm–*c*9.45pm • Royal Albert Hall

● £11–£56 *(plus booking fee')*

JULES BUCKLEY

Arooj Aftab and Friends

Arooj Aftab
Ibrahim Maalouf

BBC Symphony Orchestra
Jules Buckley *conductor*

There will be one interval

Grammy-winning artist Arooj Aftab is breaking new ground with her captivating, eclectic melting-pot of influences from jazz, folk, pop, blues and South Asian classical. For her Proms debut tonight, Aftab collaborates with Jules Buckley and the BBC Symphony Orchestra to reinvent her distinctive sound on a symphonic scale. Aftab is joined by special guests, including an opening set from French-Lebanese trumpeter, producer and composer Ibrahim Maalouf. Drawing on Latin American and Middle Eastern sounds and electronica, he believes music 'should be limitless'. A chance to encounter two richly talented, genre-curious artists.

£8 Promming tickets available for every concert

Wednesday 30 July

7.30pm–c9.35pm • Royal Albert Hall

● £10–£46 *(plus booking fee*)*

TADAAKI OTAKA

Rachmaninov's Second Piano Concerto

Bacewicz Concerto for String Orchestra 14'

Rachmaninov Piano Concerto No. 2 in C minor 33'

INTERVAL

Lutosławski Concerto for Orchestra 28'

Vadym Kholodenko *piano*

BBC National Orchestra of Wales
Tadaaki Otaka *conductor*

A romantic classic meets two 20th-century masterworks in a concert of widescreen orchestral drama. From its thunderous opening chords to its heartbreaking slow movement, Rachmaninov's Piano Concerto No. 2 is an emotional tour de force. Ukraine-born Vadym Kholodenko joins the BBC National Orchestra of Wales and Conductor Laureate Tadaaki Otaka. Framing the concerto are two orchestral showpieces: Bacewicz's vibrant *Concerto for String Orchestra* – whose motoric outer movements contrast with a sublime Andante – and the daring invention of Lutosławski's folk-inspired *Concerto for Orchestra*.

Thursday 31 July

6.30pm–c8.35pm • Royal Albert Hall

● £10–£46 *(plus booking fee*)*

MARTIN FRÖST

Rachmaninov and Copland

Barraine Symphony No. 2 17'
Copland Clarinet Concerto 18'
A. Shaw Clarinet Concerto 8'

INTERVAL

Rachmaninov Symphonic Dances 35'

Martin Fröst *clarinet*

BBC Philharmonic Orchestra
Joshua Weilerstein *conductor*

The thrum of urban America – jazz clubs and bustling sidewalks, pulsing Latin rhythms and night-time lights – runs through this Prom given by Joshua Weilerstein and the BBC Philharmonic Orchestra. Rachmaninov's enigmatic final masterpiece, the *Symphonic Dances*, blends Russian soul with bold colours from the composer's adopted homeland. Copland's Clarinet Concerto draws on the virtuoso skills of jazz legend Benny Goodman, while bandleader Artie Shaw wrote his Clarinet Concerto for his own considerable skills as a player. Elsa Barraine's tautly lyrical Symphony No. 2 opens the programme. *See page 20.*

Thursday 31 July

10.15pm–c11.30pm • Royal Albert Hall ☾

● £10–£28 *(plus booking fee*)*

TÕNU KALJUSTE

Arvo Pärt at 90

Arvo Pärt Da pacem Domine; Veni creator; Magnificat; The Deer's Cry; Für Jan van Eyck* 24'
*UK premiere

Galina Grigorjeva Svyatki – 'Spring is coming' 3'

Rachmaninov All-Night Vigil (Vespers) – 'Slava v vyshnikh Bogu'; 'Bogoroditse Devo' 6'

J. S. Bach Motet 'Ich lasse dich nicht', BWV 1165 10'

Arvo Pärt Peace upon you, Jerusalem; De profundis; Vater unser 15'

Tormis Curse upon Iron 10'

Estonian Philharmonic Chamber Choir
Tõnu Kaljuste *conductor*

There will be no interval

Sound and silence, stillness and motion are woven together in the music of Arvo Pärt. Celebrate the 90th birthday of 'the father of Holy Minimalism' with a Late-Night Prom from acclaimed Pärt interpreters Tõnu Kaljuste and the Estonian Philharmonic Chamber Choir – named one of the world's best choirs by *BBC Music Magazine*. The programme also includes excerpts from Rachmaninov's exquisite *Vespers* and music from Pärt's fellow Estonian Veljo Tormis and from Ukraine-born, Estonia-resident Galina Grigorjeva. *See pages 38–41.*

Spotlight on ...
Yunchan Lim • 1 August

Since winning the Van Cliburn International Piano Competition in 2022, aged just 18, South Korean Yunchan Lim has become nothing less than a piano superstar. It was with Rachmaninov's Piano Concerto No. 3 that he stormed to success, and – following a Proms debut with Beethoven's 'Emperor' Concerto last summer – he returns with Rachmaninov's Fourth Concerto this year. 'Rachmaninov's music should be regarded as his soul itself,' Lim explains. 'When I listen to his music, I can only hear his great, noble soul. I have played his music since childhood, but at that time I was in a hurry to imitate his own performances. Now when I play his music I try to become his soul. Rachmaninov understood the piano better than anyone else. His music is like Bach: his heart-wrenching melody, his introspective voice and his dramatic bass blend well throughout his works.' Lesser known than the Third, Rachmaninov's Fourth Concerto, Lim says, is 'my personal favourite ... For me, it evokes many different emotions and scenes: nostalgia for his hometown, receiving a love letter, even playing a card game. I hope the audience can feel that.'

How is Lim coping with his new-found fame? With modesty and self-awareness, it seems. 'You cannot judge an artist by the number of awards they have won,' he continues, 'or by the number of concerts they have performed. Take Chopin, who we love and respect, but who performed only around 30 times in his life.'

Friday 1 August
7.30pm–c9.30pm • Royal Albert Hall

● **£15–£66** (plus booking fee')

KAZUKI YAMADA

Yunchan Lim Plays Rachmaninov

John Adams The Chairman Dances — 12'

Rachmaninov Piano Concerto No. 4 in G minor — 29'

INTERVAL

Berio Sinfonia — 27'

Yunchan Lim *piano*

BBC Singers
City of Birmingham Symphony Orchestra
Kazuki Yamada *conductor*

After a 'dazzling' Proms debut last year, pianist and global phenomenon Yunchan Lim returns, joining Kazuki Yamada and the City of Birmingham Symphony Orchestra for Rachmaninov's final piano concerto. Rich in scope and ambition, tinged with the jazz rhythms and harmonies of the composer's new homeland, it's a technical tour de force. Musical visions from the New World continue in two other works: John Adams's 'foxtrot for orchestra' *The Chairman Dances*, a surreal set-piece from his hit opera *Nixon in China*, in which a young Mao Zedong dances with the future Madame Mao; and Berio's iconic *Sinfonia* (dedicated to Leonard Bernstein) – an explosive, psychedelic remix of classical music's past that asks big questions about its future. *See pages 68–71.*

Saturday 2 August
11am–c1pm • Royal Albert Hall ☀

● **£15–£66** (plus booking fee')

ERIN MORLEY

Viennese Whirl

Johann Strauss II Die Fledermaus – overture; 'Mein Herr Marquis' (Laughing Song) — 13'

Josef Strauss Brennende Liebe – polka-mazurka — 6'

Johann Strauss II Frühlingstimmen – waltz — 8'

Korngold Straussiana — 7'

Stolz Wiener Café – waltz — 6'

Dostal Fröhliches Spiel — 5'

Johann Strauss II By the Beautiful Blue Danube – waltz — 6'

and works by Lehár, Kálmán and others

Erin Morley *soprano*

BBC Concert Orchestra
Anna-Maria Helsing *conductor*

There will be one interval

Marking 200 years since the birth of 'Waltz King' Johann Strauss II, a celebration of the opulence and enchantment of Vienna's Golden Age. The Prom also features pieces by later composers inspired by the most popular dance in three-time. American soprano Erin Morley joins Anna-Maria Helsing and the BBC Concert Orchestra. *See pages 34–36.*

🖥 *Broadcast on BBC Two and BBC iPlayer this season*

Saturday 2 August

8pm–c9.30pm • Royal Albert Hall

● £15–£66 (plus booking fee')

EMILY D'ANGELO

Mahler's 'Resurrection' Symphony

Mahler Symphony No. 2 in C minor, 'Resurrection'   *80'*

Mari Eriksmoen *soprano*
Emily D'Angelo *mezzo-soprano*

Hallé Choir
Hallé Youth Choir
Hallé
Kahchun Wong *conductor*

There will be no interval

'One is battered to the ground and then raised on angel's wings to the highest heights.' Mahler's 'Resurrection' Symphony offers a panoramic vision of human existence and hope for the life beyond – suffering, redemption and renewal generated by huge orchestral and choral forces. The Hallé's new Principal Conductor Kahchun Wong directs his Manchester-based forces for the first time at the Proms, joined by two star soloists: Norwegian soprano Mari Eriksmoen and Canadian mezzo-soprano Emily D'Angelo, who makes her much-anticipated Proms debut.

Sunday 3 August

7.30pm–c9.45pm • Royal Albert Hall

◑ £11–£56 (plus booking fee')

DANIEL BARTHOLOMEW-POYSER

Soul Revolution

Trevor Nelson *presenter*

BBC Concert Orchestra
Daniel Bartholomew-Poyser *conductor*

There will be one interval

With guest vocalists, a gospel choir and renowned Radio 2 presenter Trevor Nelson, the BBC Concert Orchestra and Daniel Bartholomew-Poyser trace a path from spirituals through gospel to soul, revealing the role of these genres in supporting the Civil Rights movement. Inspirational tracks made famous by Marvin Gaye, Stevie Wonder, Nina Simone and Aretha Franklin rub shoulders with hidden gems in a celebration of music that gave a voice to disenfranchised people, fostered a sense of community – and jumped with an infectious groove.

🖳 *Broadcast on BBC Two and BBC iPlayer this season*

Every Prom is broadcast on BBC Radio 3 and BBC Sounds

Spotlight on ...

Kahchun Wong • 2 August

'Terrifying. I think that's the word to describe the beginning of Mahler's Second Symphony,' says Kahchun Wong. 'It starts in the midst of hell, and then goes through a long, beautiful and transcendental journey.' To Wong, this musical narrative of death, life and the fate of the human soul evokes epic tales from across times and cultures, from Tolkien's *The Lord of the Rings* to the ancient Indian *Ramayana* to Wu Cheng'en's 16th-century Chinese novel *Journey to the West*. 'In all of this literature you can find something in common with the scope and depth of Mahler's writing,' he says. 'We begin with catastrophe and loss, and then we go on a 90-minute journey of redemption, soul-searching and adventure. Mahler allows us, regardless of where we come from, to experience a universal kind of catharsis.'

The last seven minutes of the piece mark what is 'possibly one of the most unrivalled climaxes of classical music history,' says Wong. 'Of course, there are peaks before that, but they have to be tempered so that the musicians and the audience don't feel exhausted from climbing one Everest after another.' Instead, he will focus on drawing out the intricate details in Mahler's score to build more gradually towards an end that is, he says, 'just pure beauty. Every single performance I see musicians with tears in their eyes. It's one of those great moments. What a joy to be doing it with the Hallé, as our debut together at the Proms.'

Spotlight on ...
Natalya Romaniw • 4 August

For some, Mahler's cantata *Das klagende Lied* – a dark, Brothers Grimm-inspired tale of love, betrayal, eerie magic and justice – is the closest the composer came to opera. For Welsh soprano Natalya Romaniw, who joins three other soloists for a performance on 4 August, there are similar opportunities for a vocalist whether a work is intended for a concert hall or an opera house. 'When performing any music,' she explains, 'there has to be a narrative, even in works without a text. The voice is so wonderful in that way. It's able to convey emotion through colour, timbre and dynamics, as well as words. I approach any music as a storytelling opportunity. You're given a character's skeleton with a text, but it's wonderful to flesh it out! The only difference between concert and operatic performance is that, with the former, you don't have a costume to help you embody the character. We have to use imagination.'

Mahler wrote extensively for the voice. How does Romaniw find his vocal music? 'I've not sung this particular piece before but I've performed in his Second and Eighth Symphonies, which were both transformational experiences. The voice demonstrates everything in his music from the most delicate moments to utterly majestic and triumphant ones. In terms of his bigger moments, if you have a voice that can take on Mahler, then you just sing lyrically with your own instrument – you don't need anything more.'

Monday 4 August
7.30pm–*c*9.40pm • Royal Albert Hall

● £10–£46 *(plus booking fee*)*

RUSSELL THOMAS

Mahler and Boulez

Boulez Rituel in memoriam Bruno Maderna　　*32'*

INTERVAL

Mahler Das klagende Lied (original version, 1880)　　*65'*

Natalya Romaniw *soprano*
Jennifer Johnston *mezzo-soprano*
Russell Thomas *tenor*
James Newby *baritone*

Constanza Chorus
BBC Symphony Chorus
BBC Symphony Orchestra
Hannu Lintu *conductor*

Das klagende Lied, Mahler's musical coming-of-age, is a chilling fable of jealousy, murder and magic. An eerie woodland and a lively wedding ceremony are the centrepieces of a cantata of vast sonic imagination – a foretaste of the symphonies to come – heard here in its original three-part version. Mahler's sonic scope meets its match in the musical spectacle of Pierre Boulez's 'majestic processional' *Rituel in memoriam Bruno Maderna*. Dedicated to the composer's long-time colleague and friend, the work transforms the concert hall into a temple, in which the audience is immersed in the sounds created by eight groups of musicians. *See pages 68–71, 86.*

Tuesday 5 August
7pm–*c*9.35pm • Royal Albert Hall

● £11–£56 *(plus booking fee*)*

NIL VENDITTI

Great British Classics

Walton Coronation March 'Orb and Sceptre'　　*7'*

S. Coleridge-Taylor The Lee Shore; Isle of Beauty; The Evening Star　　*9'*

A. Coleridge-Taylor The Shepherd　　*4'*

Vaughan Williams The Lark Ascending　　*13'*

Britten Four Sea Interludes from 'Peter Grimes'　　*16'*

INTERVAL

Mathias Dance Overture　　*6'*

John Rutter new work　　*c8'*
BBC commission: world premiere

G. Williams Elegy for Strings　　*7'*

Elgar 'Enigma' Variations　　*31'*

Liya Petrova *violin*

BBC Singers
BBC National Orchestra of Wales
Nil Venditti *conductor*

A celebration of Britain's land- and sea-scapes. Hear the soaring flight of Vaughan Williams's *The Lark Ascending* as well as the many moods of the North Sea as it meets Suffolk shingle in Britten's *Four Sea Interludes from 'Peter Grimes'*.

🖵 *Broadcast on BBC Two and BBC iPlayer this season*

Wednesday 6 August

7.30pm–c9.40pm • Royal Albert Hall

● £15–£66 (plus booking fee')

DOROTTYA LÁNG

Beethoven and Bartók from Budapest

Beethoven Symphony No. 7 in A major   36'

INTERVAL

Bartók Duke Bluebeard's Castle   55'
(sung in Hungarian, with English surtitles)

Dorottya Láng Judith
Krisztián Cser Duke Bluebeard

Budapest Festival Orchestra
Iván Fischer conductor

From light into darkness: Beethoven's ebullient Symphony No. 7 – 'glorious wine for the human spirit' – gives way to the shadows and horrors of Bartók's Duke Bluebeard's Castle. Iván Fischer and the Budapest Festival Orchestra bring Hungary's greatest opera to the Royal Albert Hall. The legend of Bluebeard and his young wife Judith – whose persistent curiosity forces the Duke to reveal the secrets hidden behind the locked doors of his castle – comes to idiomatic life in the hands of a Hungarian cast. See pages 82–84.

Thursday 7 August

7.30pm–c9.35pm • Royal Albert Hall

● £11–£56 (plus booking fee')

DOMINGO HINDOYAN

Dvořák's 'New World' Symphony

Adolphus Hailstork An American Port of Call   9'
European premiere

Jennifer Higdon Blue Cathedral   11'

Arturo Márquez Concierto de otoño   19'

INTERVAL

Dvořák Symphony No. 9 in E minor, 'From the New World'   40'

Pacho Flores trumpet

Percussionists from Liverpool Philharmonic Youth Company and In Harmony Liverpool
Royal Liverpool Philharmonic Orchestra
Domingo Hindoyan conductor

A musical postcard from America. Dvořák's 'New World' Symphony is charged with nostalgia, its lyrical warmth offering a striking contrast to the zesty contemporary drama of Adolphus Hailstok's An American Port of Call – a musical portrait of a busy port city – and the transcendent peace of Jennifer Higdon's Blue Cathedral – 'a symbolic doorway into and out of this world'. Venezuelan trumpet virtuoso Pacho Flores is the soloist in Arturo Márquez's vibrant and tune-filled Concierto de otoño. See pages 78–81.

🖥 Broadcast on BBC Four and BBC iPlayer this season

Spotlight on ...

Pacho Flores • 7 August

Venezuelan trumpeter Pacho Flores's Proms performance on 7 August will be, he says, a meeting of old friends. He and conductor Domingo Hindoyan go back to their teenage years: 'We both trained in El Sistema,' Flores explains, 'so we've known each other for about 25 years. And when Domingo joined the Royal Liverpool Philharmonic Orchestra as Chief Conductor I got the chance to be Artist in Residence. So I've done lots of projects with them – and we have more planned. I now say that Liverpool is my home in England, and that they're my family. I feel a lot of emotion about this concert.'

The piece Flores is performing – the Concierto de otoño by Arturo Márquez – has strong personal connections, too. 'I've also known Arturo since I was a teenager. He wrote this "Autumn Concerto" for me in 2016, when he was 66, because he felt that he was in the autumn of his life. I've since played it more than 80 times around the world.' The piece captures Flores's exuberant personality in its distinctively Latin rhythms and sultry harmonies. It also enables Flores to engage directly with listeners in the solo cadenza. 'I like to improvise there, make some connection with the audience, even send kisses through the trumpet. It's part of my musical personality: as 21st-century musicians, we have to find happiness and connection with our music, to show listeners that classical music is enjoyable and beautiful.'

Spotlight on …
Anna Lapwood • 8 August

'It's something I've been wanting to try for years.' Anna Lapwood is talking about the all-night Prom on 8 August, which sees performers and audience alike given rare night-time access to the Royal Albert Hall. Lapwood herself will be at the centre of the evening – as organist, conductor and guest curator – and, she explains, the idea sprang from her own personal experiences. 'I'm rehearsing on the Hall's organ about two or three nights a week at the moment. It sometimes seems like a bizarre novelty that organists have to do these overnight rehearsals, but we all do. It's when a venue's organ is available for the longest period of time. I love it, though – you get to know the heart of the building, and also the people who are still around working during the night. We're trying to capture some of that childlike joy and excitement – almost like *Night at the Museum* – which I don't think ever really wears off.' Despite the event's nocturnal time-frame, Lapwood is clear: 'We very consciously don't want it to be: come to the Royal Albert Hall to sleep. We'll have a shape and flow to the event that allows for restful periods, but also brings the energy up at certain times. Some moments will feel more like a traditional concert, but we're also planning to have sections where listeners can engage with the performance in different ways. I'm just going to have to figure out managing sleep and rehearsals for myself so that I get into that different time zone …'

Friday 8 August
6pm–c8.05pm • Royal Albert Hall

● **£10–£46** *(plus booking fee')*

BEATRICE RANA

Rachmaninov's 'Paganini' Variations

Dukas La Péri – Poème dansé   18'
Rachmaninov Rhapsody on a
Theme of Paganini   25'

INTERVAL

Bartók The Miraculous Mandarin   32'

Beatrice Rana *piano*

BBC Singers
BBC Symphony Orchestra
Josep Pons *conductor*

Desire, brutality and the supernatural are shaken together in the orchestral kaleidoscope of Bartók's ballet *The Miraculous Mandarin*. Josep Pons conducts the BBC Symphony Orchestra in the last of Bartók's three great music-theatre scores, an electrifying fusion of folk music and modernism. Angular brilliance gives way to exotic, Impressionistic colours in Dukas's exotic 'danced poem' *La Péri*. 'Remarkable' Italian pianist Beatrice Rana is the soloist in Rachmaninov's thrilling *Rhapsody on a Theme of Paganini*.

Friday 8 August
11pm–7am • Royal Albert Hall

● **£11–£56** *(plus booking fee')*

From Dark Till Dawn

Artists to include:

Anna Lapwood *organ/conductor*

Barokksolistene
Bjarte Eike *violin/director*
Pembroke College Chapel Choir
Anastasia Kobekina *cello*
Hayato Sumino *piano*

There will be two intervals

Experience the Royal Albert Hall at its most magical, with an intimate after-hours Prom amid the night stars and beneath the Hall's grand dome. Celebrated organist and TikTok star Anna Lapwood is guest curator and brings choral classics with her choir from Pembroke College. Among the other boundary-crossing artists are dynamic Norwegian ensemble Barokksolistene and director Bjarte Eike, who create a tavern-like mood with traditional British and Scandinavian songs as part of their Nordic Alehouse Session. Following her Proms debut last year Russian cellist Anastasia Kobekina returns with a set of solo Bach; and Chopin Competition semi-finalist – and YouTube sensation – Hayato Sumino makes his Proms debut. A unique musical journey extending from the nocturnal hours to beyond the dawn chorus.

Saturday 9 August

7pm–c9.15pm • Royal Albert Hall

● £15–£66 (plus booking fee*)

DALIA STASEVSKA

The Planets and Star Wars

John Williams Star Wars – suite   25'
Caroline Shaw The Observatory   14'
INTERVAL
Holst The Planets   51'

National Youth Orchestra
Dalia Stasevska conductor

Britain's most talented teenagers present a concert of intergalactic musical giants. Expect moons and meteor showers, spaceships, stars and lightsabers from the National Youth Orchestra and Dalia Stasevska. The many worlds of Holst's *The Planets*, including the mysterious beauty of 'Neptune' and rousing 'Jupiter' theme, meet the music from John Williams's mighty *Star Wars* soundtracks, plus Pulitzer Prize-winner Caroline Shaw's piece inspired by sci-fi and some sky-gazing at the Griffin Observatory in Los Angeles. *See page 98.*

🖵 *Broadcast on BBC Two and BBC iPlayer this season*

£8 Promming tickets available for every concert

Sunday 10 August

11am – c12.15pm • Royal Albert Hall   ☀

● £10–£28 (plus booking fee*)

TESS JACKSON

Relaxed Prom: The Planets

John Williams Star Wars – suite   15'
Caroline Shaw The Observatory – excerpt   5'
Holst The Planets – Mars; Venus; Mercury; Jupiter   27'

National Youth Orchestra
Tess Jackson conductor
Linton Stephens presenter

There will be no interval

AD *Audio-described by Timna Fibert*
BSL *British Sign Language-interpreted*

A chance to hear some of the music of last night's Prom – including excerpts from Holst's awe-inspiring *The Planets* and music from John Williams's mighty *Star Wars* soundtracks – in a relaxed and informal environment, presented by Radio 3's Linton Stephens and musicians from the National Youth Orchestra. *See page 98.*

This is a relaxed performance, designed to suit individuals or groups who feel more comfortable attending concerts in an informal environment. There is a relaxed attitude to noise and audience members are free to leave and re-enter the auditorium at any point. Chill-out areas offer a space for anyone who needs some quiet time before or during the performance. For full details, visit bbc.co.uk/proms.

Sunday 10 August

7.30pm–c9.30pm • Royal Albert Hall

● £11–£56 (plus booking fee*)

AIGUL AKHMETSHINA

Edward Gardner Conducts the LPO

Sibelius The Oceanides   11'
Tippett The Rose Lake   29'
INTERVAL
Ravel Shéhérazade   17'
Debussy La mer   23'

Aigul Akhmetshina mezzo-soprano

London Philharmonic Orchestra
Edward Gardner conductor

Waves play and waterfalls plunge, the still surface of a lake reflects the midday sun and an ocean duets with the wind in a concert with saltwater on its breath. Edward Gardner conducts the London Philharmonic Orchestra in a programme of 20th-century orchestral sound-pictures. The mercurial moods of Debussy's *La mer* and rolling waters of Sibelius's *The Oceanides* find answer in the gentle rolling harbour of Ravel's song-cycle *Shéhérazade*, performed – in a Proms debut – by mezzo-soprano Aigul Akhmetshina. Tippett's last major work takes us inland to discover a glowing 'lake full of song'. *See pages 22–26.*

Spotlight on ...
Ryan Bancroft • 11 August

Ryan Bancroft brings the BBC National Orchestra of Wales to the Proms twice this year with two very different concerts. 'I was quite late coming to Mahler's Third Symphony,' he admits of his first performance, on 11 August. 'But it brings out the best in all of us who encounter it – it's a magnified vision of the world that explores wild and fantastical nature, and also plumbs the depths of lamentation and bliss. As a performer, that can be seen as a tall order – but it's one I'll willingly return to time and time again.'

Two iconic Soviet composers bookend the concert on 15 August. 'I was fortunate enough to work with Sofia Gubaidulina at a very young age,' he explains. 'Her *Revue Music* is a wonderfully strange mix of modernistic orchestral music and extremely groovy jazz – it's a piece that hits you in the face when you least expect it.' Shostakovich's Symphony No. 13, however, takes a far darker theme: the Nazi massacre of Jews at Babi Yar, near Kyiv, in 1941. 'The primary challenge is embracing the harsh reality of the piece,' Bancroft observes. 'It's bleak, sardonic and sobering – much like what's happening in our world today. Though the piece depicts despair, we must approach it beautifully and with compassion. I'd never dream of imposing a grand meaning on a listener, as the experience can and should be quite personal, but I do believe we need beauty and compassion more than ever.'

Monday 11 August
7pm–c8.45pm • Royal Albert Hall

⬤ £11–£56 *(plus booking fee')*

BETH TAYLOR

Mahler's Third

Mahler Symphony No. 3 in D minor   96'

Beth Taylor *mezzo-soprano*

CBSO Children's Chorus
BBC National Chorus of Wales (upper voices)
Welsh National Opera Chorus (upper voices)
BBC National Orchestra of Wales
Orchestre National de Bretagne
Ryan Bancroft *conductor*

There will be no interval

'A symphony should be like the world,' Mahler said, 'it should embrace everything.' Nowhere does this vision come more powerfully to life than in his mighty Symphony No. 3, an intricate, joyful tapestry of man, nature and heaven. The work opens in heavy summer heat and closes in rapt tranquillity in a sublime finale, animated in between by marches, dances and birdsong. Ryan Bancroft brings together the BBC National Orchestra of Wales and the Orchestre National de Bretagne, joined by the CBSO Children's Chorus, the upper voices of the Welsh National Opera Chorus and BBC National Chorus of Wales and mezzo-soprano Beth Taylor.

Tuesday 12 August
7pm–c8.30pm • Royal Albert Hall

⬤ £26–£86 *(plus booking fee')*

ANOUSHKA SHANKAR

Anoushka Shankar: 'Chapters'

Anoushka Shankar

London Contemporary Orchestra
Robert Ames *conductor*

There will be no interval

Multi-Grammy-nominated sitar virtuoso and composer Anoushka Shankar returns to the Proms for the world-premiere performance of music from her three 'Chapter' albums, tracing her musical and geographical journeys. She is joined by Robert Ames and the London Contemporary Orchestra to perform new orchestral arrangements of the trilogy – *Forever, For Now, How Dark It Is Before Dawn* and *We Return To Light. See pages 64–66.*

🖥 *Broadcast on BBC Four and BBC iPlayer this season*

Tuesday 12 August

10.15pm–c11.30pm • Royal Albert Hall ☾

● £10–£28 *(plus booking fee')*

Late Night

THE CAVEMEN.

The Cavemen.

The Cavemen.

There will be no interval

Before there was Afrobeat there was highlife – a joyful, good-times Ghanaian musical style that took on a new gloss in 1960s Nigeria. Praised for their 'bewitching, colourful and easy-listening grooves', Nigerian sensations Kingsley Okorie and Benjamin James bring their distinctive brand of 'highlife fusion' to the BBC Proms. Blending Igbo highlife – all bright horns, plucked guitar riffs and pulsing percussion – with jazz and soul, the brothers launched their careers with the influential 2020 album *ROOTS* (recorded in their living room) and have since collaborated with everyone from Wizkid to Angélique Kidjo and Davido.

Every Prom is broadcast on BBC Radio 3 and BBC Sounds

Wednesday 13 August

7.30pm–c9.40pm • Royal Albert Hall

● £10–£46 *(plus booking fee')*

EVA OLLIKAINEN

Boléro and The Rite of Spring

Varèse Intégrales	12'
Anna Thorvaldsdottir Before we fall (Cello Concerto)	26'
BBC co-commission: UK premiere	
Ravel Boléro	13'
INTERVAL	
Stravinsky The Rite of Spring	33'

Johannes Moser *cello*

BBC Symphony Orchestra
Eva Ollikainen *conductor*

Feel the beat. From the primal, hypnotic dances of Stravinsky's *The Rite of Spring* to the sensual throb of Ravel's *Boléro* and the edgy thrum and twitch of Varèse's *Intégrales*, the BBC Symphony Orchestra and Eva Ollikainen get the musical pulse racing. They're joined by 'stupendous' German-Canadian cellist Johannes Moser for the UK premiere of Anna Thorvaldsdottir's *Before we fall* – a work that teeters on the edge of 'a multitude of opposites', torn between lyricism and distorted energy. *See pages 22–26, 94–95.*

Spotlight on …

Johannes Moser • 13 August

When Johannes Moser first saw the score for *Before we fall*, its notes leapt out at him with near-physical force. Composer Anna Thorvaldsdottir sends the solo cellist forwards, he says, like 'a gladiator into the arena, and has the gladiator converse with the orchestra'. That conversation reveals 'the beauty of the cello, but also the fragile and humble qualities that come with it'. Here the soloist is 'a failed hero' who teeters on an edge above the powerful sonic maw of the orchestra. 'Sometimes you have compositions that are great on paper, and then you bring them into the real world and they don't have any sense of three-dimensionality,' says Moser. 'When Thorvaldsdottir composes, she conducts through the music to explore how it will feel in space. That physical approach makes her work so accessible for people from all walks of life, because you can really feel the music.'

Moser premieres *Before we fall* in May but this Prom marks his first collaboration with the BBC Symphony Orchestra and Eva Ollikainen. Is it intimidating to navigate unfamiliar orchestras, conductors and scores all at once? 'It widens my horizons and introduces me to new people, which I love,' he says. 'To really know what is possible with the material, it's great to work with it in different settings, with different players. It's like moulding one piece of clay in multiple new ways. Then the piece starts to come alive.'

Spotlight on …
Joe Hisaishi • 14 August

When Joe Hisaishi wrote *The End of the World* after visiting Ground Zero in New York in 2007, he did so, he says, 'in recognition of the souls lost and affected' in the 9/11 terrorist attacks. Optimistic that more peaceful and unified times would follow, in his second movement he juxtaposed cheering sounds inspired by the Arab world and the bustle of New York City. 'But it has been 24 years and things have not become better,' he says. 'I felt such a shock when I performed this piece in Tokyo last year as I recognised this.'

Just as Hisaishi's work was born of conflict and catastrophe, so Reich's *The Desert Music* 'was inspired by the desert of New Mexico's Tularosa Basin, where atomic bomb tests were conducted,' says Hisaishi. 'This year is the 80th anniversary of the end of the Second World War and it looks as if another war could break out at any moment.' Nevertheless, he clarifies, he does not mean for this performance to be an anti-war statement. Rather, he says, 'I want it to be an energetic and positive concert that says: "Let's not lose sight of ourselves in this situation, and let's live strong with solidarity!" It is the greatest pleasure for me to perform my own composition at the historic BBC Proms, alongside the work of Steve Reich, a composer whom I deeply respect and admire. I look forward to presenting this programme of Minimalist music in the grand acoustic of the Royal Albert Hall.'

Thursday 14 August
7.30pm–c9.25pm • Royal Albert Hall

● £26–£86 *(plus booking fee')*

JOHN HOLIDAY

Joe Hisaishi and Steve Reich

Joe Hisaishi The End of the World   31'

INTERVAL

Steve Reich The Desert Music   48'

John Holiday *counter-tenor*

BBC Singers
National Youth Voices
Philharmonia Chorus
Royal Philharmonic Orchestra
Joe Hisaishi *conductor*

Legendary Studio Ghibli composer Joe Hisaishi makes his Proms debut. On the 80th anniversary of the bombings of Hiroshima and Nagasaki, he conducts the Royal Philharmonic Orchestra in two large-scale works exploring themes of destruction and loss. The cinematic soundscapes of Hisaishi's own *The End of the World* are set against the restless electric pulse and shimmer of Steve Reich's *The Desert Music* – a scorched-earth vision of a post-nuclear wasteland.

£8 Promming tickets available for every concert

Friday 15 August
7.30pm–c9.50pm • Royal Albert Hall

● £15–£66 *(plus booking fee')*

BENJAMIN GROSVENOR

Benjamin Grosvenor Plays Ravel

Sofia Gubaidulina Revue Music for Symphony Orchestra and Jazz Band   10'
UK premiere

Ravel Piano Concerto in G major   23'

INTERVAL

Shostakovich Symphony No. 13 in B flat minor, 'Babi Yar'   59'

Benjamin Grosvenor *piano*
Alexander Vinogradov *bass*

Synergy Vocals
BBC National Chorus of Wales (lower voices)
Welsh National Opera Chorus (lower voices)
BBC National Orchestra of Wales
Ryan Bancroft *conductor*

A jazz band and a symphony orchestra meet in the zany groovings of Sofia Gubaidulina's *Revue Music for Symphony Orchestra and Jazz Band* – part of a concert that brings these two sound-worlds together. Jazz is represented by the syncopated brilliance of Ravel's Piano Concerto in G major, performed by Proms favourite and former BBC Radio 3 New Generation Artist Benjamin Grosvenor. Shostakovich supplies the symphony – the snarling, sometimes shockingly tender 'Babi Yar', bearing witness to the horrors of a Nazi massacre of Jews in Soviet Ukraine. *See pages 22–26, 58–62.*

Saturday 16 August

7pm–c9.10pm • Royal Albert Hall

● £15–£66 (plus booking fee*)

Sunday 17 August

11am–1.10pm • Royal Albert Hall ☀

● £15–£66 (plus booking fee*)

Shostakovich's Fifth by Heart

A musical and dramatic exploration
of Shostakovich's Symphony No. 5   c40'

INTERVAL

Shostakovich Symphony No. 5
in D minor (performed from memory)   51'

Aurora Orchestra
Nicholas Collon conductor

AD Audio-described by Timna Fibert
BSL British Sign Language-interpreted

Explore a symphony from the inside out.
Nicholas Collon and the Aurora Orchestra
reflect this year's Shostakovich anniversary
with a Prom that takes the audience under the
hood of a 20th-century masterpiece and into
the mind of the man who made it. Actors join
the Aurora players to bring to life a symphony
born in the shadow of Stalin's regime – music
on the edge of life and death, written by a
composer treading a dangerous line between
political obedience and artistic defiance. *See
pages 58–62.*

🖵 *Broadcast on BBC Four and BBC iPlayer this season*

Every Prom is
broadcast on
BBC Radio 3 and
BBC Sounds

Sunday 17 August

7.30pm–c9pm • Royal Albert Hall

● £11–£56 (plus booking fee*)

HERVÉ NIQUET

Le Concert Spirituel

Striggio
Mass 'Ecco sì beato giorno'   29'
Motet 'Ecce beatam lucem'   8'

*Interspersed with works by Benevolo, Corteccia
and Palestrina*

Le Concert Spirituel
Hervé Niquet conductor
There will be no interval

Before there was Tallis's mighty *Spem in alium*
there was Striggio's 40-part Mass: a sumptuous
Renaissance epic in surround sound. Lost for
centuries, it received its contemporary premiere
at the 2007 Proms. Now it returns, in the expert
hands of period specialists Le Concert Spirituel
under Hervé Niquet. Their musical ritual – a
concert recreation of a festal Mass – also
includes the 'heavenly harmony' of the equally
striking (and supersized) motet *Ecce beatam
lucem*, music by 16th- and 17th-century Italian
composers Benevolo and Corteccia, as well as
motets by Palestrina, whose 500th anniversary
falls this year.

Spotlight on ...

Nicholas Collon
16 & 17 August

'Shostakovich's Fifth Symphony is a
uniquely fascinating piece,' says Nicholas
Collon. 'We're going to use the fact that
we've memorised it to really dig into the
details of its background – not just the
history and the social and political context,
but the music itself, the notes, the way
Shostakovich orchestrated it, its brilliance.
And we won't do it in a dry way. It's not
like the orchestra is sitting there playing
excerpts from behind music stands. We can
use the stage – and use it dramatically.'

In the first half of the concert Collon and
his colleagues will call on words, acting
and musical excerpts to explore
Shostakovich's experience of composing
under the scrutiny of Stalin and his Soviet
artistic committees in the 1930s. They will
then perform the complete symphony from
memory in the second half. Is it a difficult
work to memorise? 'I actually think it is
quite easy,' he says. 'There aren't millions
of notes, the textures are quite bare, and
the scales are pretty obvious. The hardest
thing about Shostakovich's Fifth is that
the solos and violin writing are very quiet,
high and exposed. But the music suits
the Royal Albert Hall really well. It has
extraordinarily intimate moments, and
big moments that can terrify and create
all sorts of emotions. It's very powerful
and moving. Perhaps appreciating the
struggle that Shostakovich went through
on behalf of his art will make listening to
it an even richer experience.'

Spotlight on ...
Carolina López Moreno
19 August

'Singing Puccini is like a drug,' says Carolina López Moreno. 'You are so high afterwards, because it's so gorgeous and special.' It is music, she says, that can be understood by anyone, whatever their age, culture or experience of opera. 'I see all kinds of faces and emotions in the audience when I perform it. They go through everything with you.'

In this Prom, she expects tears to flow as she sings the title-role of *Suor Angelica*, who sacrifices everything for her son and then, learning of his death, takes her own life. 'It is heartbreakingly beautiful. When I first studied it, I cried so much.' No longer do those tears make her voice break, she says: now they only add to the beauty and colour of the music.

López Moreno thinks that her performance will be especially powerful with Sir Antonio Pappano by her side. 'When he conducts, it's like honey for the vocal cords,' she says. 'He understands voices, he breathes with you. It's like when you have a conversation with someone who inspires you. You get the feeling that you can fly. You think you can do anything. It's like an explosion of emotions.' That feeling will help her to perform a work that, she says, is 'vocally so difficult. Puccini doesn't want you to be a singer. You have to scream, and to feel every emotion, to get all of the beautiful colours he wants. He wants you to tell a story, with every cell of your body.'

Monday 18 August
7.30pm–c9.45pm • Royal Albert Hall

● £10–£46 *(plus booking fee¹)*

SIR RODERICK WILLIAMS

Elder Conducts 'A Mass of Life'

Delius A Mass of Life   100'
(sung in German, with English surtitles)

Jennifer Davis *soprano*
Claudia Huckle *mezzo-soprano*
David Butt Philip *tenor*
Roderick Williams *baritone*

BBC Symphony Chorus
London Philharmonic Choir
BBC Symphony Orchestra
Sir Mark Elder *conductor*

There will be one interval

'No other English composer offers more beauty in sound,' Thomas Beecham said of Delius. There's no more extravagant, impassioned or overwhelming a canvas for that beauty than *A Mass of Life*. Taking Nietzsche's rapturous prose-poem *Also sprach Zarathustra* as a starting point, Delius imagined a secular Mass – a cantata for orchestra, chorus and soloists celebrating the transcendent power and triumph of the human spirit in the face of death. Sir Mark Elder conducts the BBC Symphony Orchestra, with soloists including baritone Roderick Williams and tenor David Butt Philip. *See page 56.*

Tuesday 19 August
7.30pm–c9.25pm • Royal Albert Hall

● £26–£86 *(plus booking fee¹)*

SIR ANTONIO PAPPANO

Pappano Conducts Puccini and Strauss

R. Strauss Die Frau ohne Schatten – Symphonic Fantasy   22'

INTERVAL

Puccini Suor Angelica   60'
(sung in Italian, with English surtitles)

Carolina López Moreno *Sister Angelica*
Kseniia Nikolaieva *Princess*
Elena Zilio *Monitress*
Angela Schisano *Mistress of the novices*
Sarah Dufresne *Sister Genovieffa*

Tiffin Choir
London Symphony Chorus
London Symphony Orchestra
Sir Antonio Pappano *conductor*

Two of the 20th-century's most powerful operas come together in a concert by Sir Antonio Pappano and the London Symphony Orchestra. Motherhood – longed-for or feared, inevitable or impossible – is the thread binding the devastating melodrama of Puccini's one-act *Suor Angelica* to Strauss's darkly ambiguous fable *Die Frau ohne Schatten* ('The Woman without a Shadow'), each a battle for humanity and its future. Soprano Carolina López Moreno stars as Puccini's tragic Sister Angelica, whose past conceals a terrible secret. *See pages 82–84.*

Wednesday 20 August

7.30pm–c9.50pm • Royal Albert Hall

● £11–£56 *(plus booking fee*)*

SANTTU-MATIAS ROUVALI

Bruce Liu Plays Tchaikovsky

Gabriela Ortiz Antrópolis   10'

Tchaikovsky Piano Concerto No. 2
in G major   44'

INTERVAL

Mussorgsky, orch. Ravel
Pictures at an Exhibition   35'

Bruce Liu *piano*

Philharmonia Orchestra
Santtu-Matias Rouvali *conductor*

Chopin Piano Competition-winner Bruce
Liu – hailed for the 'breathtaking beauty' of
his playing – makes his Proms debut with
Tchaikovsky's rarely performed Second Piano
Concerto. He joins the Philharmonia Orchestra
and Principal Conductor Santtu-Matias Rouvali
for a work that balances the intimacy of chamber
music with huge scope and virtuosity. Take a
visit to Mexico City's cabarets and dance halls in
Gabriela Ortiz's *Antrópolis* – a vivid homage to
urban nightlife – while Mussorgsky's *Pictures at
an Exhibition* conjures an orchestral kaleidoscope
of strange scenes and images, climaxing with
the splendour of the Great Gate of Kyiv.

Thursday 21 August

7.30pm–c9.50pm • Royal Albert Hall

● £15–£66 *(plus booking fee*)*

JASMIN WHITE

Beethoven's Ninth

Bent Sørensen Evening Land   13'

Anna Clyne The Years   20'

INTERVAL

Beethoven Symphony No. 9
in D minor, 'Choral'   65'

Clara Cecilie Thomsen *soprano*
Jasmin White *contralto*
Issachah Savage *tenor*
Adam Palka *bass*

Danish National Concert Choir
Danish National Symphony Orchestra
Fabio Luisi *conductor*

A concert of musical roars and whispers.
A childhood memory inspires Bent Sørensen's
Evening Land – a sonic view from a window onto
the calm, silent landscape of rural Denmark.
Inspired by the isolation of the Covid-19
lockdowns, Anna Clyne's *The Years* explores
ideas of solitude and the passing of time.
Written when Beethoven was progressively
losing his hearing, the Ninth Symphony is
a monumental statement of defiant hope,
climaxing in a musical shout of joy. Fabio Luisi
conducts the Danish National Symphony
Orchestra in a programme that charts the
extremes of human experience and emotion.
See pages 78–81.

🖥 *Broadcast on BBC Four and BBC iPlayer this season*

Spotlight on ...
Bruce Liu • 20 August

AUG
|
21
AUG

Tchaikovsky's Second Piano Concerto
may not be as well known as his First but,
to Bruce Liu, it is 'equally brilliant and even
more unique'. It is, he says, 'a hidden gem
that has given me something fresh to push
my musical development, to help me find
my own path'. He has had to learn, most
of all, to reimagine the piano as part of
the orchestra, to bring out all the music's
harp-like arpeggios and instrumental
characteristics, and to make the piano sing.
'That's the biggest challenge, because
the piano does not sing naturally,' he
says. 'It's not part of our body, it's an
external object, and it's very percussive.'

Liu first performed this concerto with the
Philharmonia Orchestra for his UK debut
in 2022. He is delighted to be playing it
with the orchestra again. 'Santtu-Matias
Rouvali is not only a great artist, but also
a great friend. To be in such good company,
with an orchestra that I trust and love,
are the best possible conditions for my
Proms debut,' he says. Does that mean he
will be nerve-free? 'I am always nervous,
especially before I go on stage!' he laughs.
'But I'm not too worried, because I think
that means I still have something new to
say. If I become completely confident, it will
mean that I am just repeating a process,
which is a danger for the music.' Above all,
he wants to transport his audience from
the Royal Albert Hall, for the time they
share together, 'into some different world'.

BBC.CO.UK/PROMS   **129**

Spotlight on …
Dalia Stasevska • 22 August

'I see a lot of similarities between Thomas de Hartmann's Violin Concerto and Górecki's Third Symphony,' says Dalia Stasevska. 'Both are laments about war and loss, and use music to reflect.' Their significance to her deepened after she visited war-torn Ukraine and after the birth of her first child in 2023. 'Now I understand on a very different level what the pain means,' she says. 'The pain of losing something. For me, this is going to be an emotional concert.'

The concerto is a phenomenal product of 1940s war-torn Ukraine, says Stasevska, written at a time that bears a 'shocking resemblance to our own. It's so current. And when a country is fighting for its freedom, preserving and protecting the art and culture that define its identity becomes vital.' That is why to preserve Ukrainian culture, and to make it visible outside Ukraine, has, she says, become 'a project so close to my heart'.

Will there be moments of light in a programme so filled with tragedy? 'Music is the light!' says Stasevska. 'Music-making gives me the energy and courage not to be paralysed, but to believe in good and to focus on helping whoever needs it, to get through this and to win. We all experience music individually, but at the same time it's a communal experience that gives us courage not to look away, not to be silent, and to somehow believe that together we can move mountains. That is the most important message of this concert.'

Friday 22 August

7.30pm–c9.45pm • Royal Albert Hall

⬤ £11–£56 *(plus booking fee*)*

JOSHUA BELL

Symphony of Sorrowful Songs

J. S. Bach, orch. Respighi Three Chorales – No. 1: 'Nun komm, der Heiden Heiland'   *6'*

T. de Hartmann Violin Concerto   *30'*
UK premiere

INTERVAL

Górecki Symphony No. 3, 'Symphony of Sorrowful Songs'   *55'*

Joshua Bell *violin*
Francesca Chiejina *soprano*

BBC Symphony Orchestra
Dalia Stasevska *conductor*

'Perhaps people find something they need in this piece … something they were missing.' Henryk Górecki's 'Symphony of Sorrowful Songs' translates a century's loss and pain into sound, gathering up the broken pieces – of history, prayer and poetry – and giving them a home in music that's as much a requiem as a symphony. Joshua Bell is the soloist in Ukraine-born composer Thomas de Hartmann's emotive, cinematic Violin Concerto, a lament for the Nazi destruction of his homeland. The concert opens with Respighi's warmly expansive reworking of an organ chorale prelude by J. S. Bach.

Saturday 23 August

11am–c12.40pm • Royal Albert Hall   ☀

⬤ £11–£56 *(plus booking fee*)*

ANDRÁS SCHIFF

András Schiff Plays Bach

J. S. Bach The Art of Fugue   *90'*

Sir András Schiff *piano*
Schaghajegh Nosrati *piano*

There will be no interval

'The greatest work by the greatest composer who ever lived.' That's how the celebrated pianist Sir András Schiff has described Bach's *The Art of Fugue*. Following acclaimed Proms performances of *The Well-Tempered Clavier* and the 'Goldberg' Variations, Schiff returns to the Proms for a musical high point of his career-long relationship with Bach's music. Here he squares up to a musical enigma, a cycle left unfinished at the composer's death that represents the most complex, inventive, intimate and joyful act of creation. He's joined for one of the work's fugues by German pianist and long-time collaborator Schaghajegh Nosrati.

£8 Promming tickets available for every concert

Saturday 23 August

8pm–c10.10pm • Royal Albert Hall

● £26–£86 *(plus booking fee')*

KLAUS MÄKELÄ

Mäkelä Conducts Mahler's Fifth

Berio Rendering   *25'*

INTERVAL

Mahler Symphony No. 5   *68'*

Royal Concertgebouw Orchestra
Klaus Mäkelä *conductor*

'Mahler that risks nothing is not worth hearing,'
Klaus Mäkelä has declared. Still in his twenties,
the electrifying Finnish conductor already
leads top orchestras in Oslo and Paris, with
Chicago and Amsterdam soon to come. Hear
him at the Proms for the first time as Chief
Conductor Designate of the mighty Royal
Concertgebouw Orchestra. Mahler's Fifth
Symphony is a tumultuous journey from the
darkness of a funeral march to brilliant light
via the famous Adagietto – the tenderest
musical love letter in the repertoire. It sits
alongside Berio's delicate 'rendering' of
Schubert's unfinished D major Symphony,
a musical palimpsest and sonic fantasy.
See pages 68–71.

🖵 *Broadcast on BBC Four and BBC iPlayer this season*

Sunday 24 August

2pm–c4pm • Royal Albert Hall

● £26–£86 *(plus booking fee')*

JANINE JANSEN

Mäkelä Conducts Mozart, Prokofiev & Bartók

Mozart Symphony No. 31
in D major, 'Paris'   *17'*

Prokofiev Violin Concerto No. 1
in D major   *22'*

INTERVAL

Bartók Concerto for Orchestra   *36'*

Janine Jansen *violin*

Royal Concertgebouw Orchestra
Klaus Mäkelä *conductor*

For their second concert, Klaus Mäkelä
and Amsterdam's Royal Concertgebouw
Orchestra are joined by celebrated violinist
Janine Jansen – back at the Proms for the
first time in over a decade as soloist in
Prokofiev's effervescent Violin Concerto No. 1.
A lyrical refuge from the storm of the Russian
Revolution, the concerto stands in contrast to
Bartók's *Concerto for Orchestra* – another heir
of conflict, but one that grapples and wrestles
with darkness with thrilling virtuosity. Mozart's
'Paris' Symphony is no less of an orchestral
showcase: a musical calling card from an
ambitious 22-year-old determined to dazzle.

Spotlight on …

Katy Woolley, RCO Principal
Horn • 24 August

Katy Woolley loves to play her French
horn in an orchestra in, she says, what feels
like 'the safety of the shadow'. There she
feels like a chameleon, sometimes playing
to complement the strings, the brass or
the winds, at others enjoying a more
soloistic line. Her first performance of the
long, exposed solo in the third movement
of Mahler's Fifth Symphony, around a
decade ago, launched her far from her
comfort zone. 'It's a very soloistic line that
goes from a Germanic celebratory dance
to extreme desperation,' she says. 'On
stage before we started, I just turned
around to the second horn and said, "I've
got really sweaty feet". I was so nervous!
I remember shaking through the first
line. It's so well written that once you're
in the flow you just go with it. But I didn't
know that, the first time I performed it.'

Do the nerves ever return, now that she
has played it more often? 'Every time!' she
laughs. 'There's no way I'm escaping that
adrenaline kick. But if you practise knowing
that's going to happen, adrenaline can
focus and enhance whatever you've been
working on.' Nowadays, to play Mahler's
Fifth is an experience that Woolley is always
keen to repeat. She is looking forward to
performing it with her orchestra 14 times
this concert season. 'It gives you the chance
to explore the human experience and to
wonder about life, about love, about loss.'
'Every single note has deep meaning.'

Spotlight on ...
Hilary Hahn • 26 August

'It's such a contagious piece,' says Hilary Hahn of Dvořák's Violin Concerto. 'It's just so much fun to play. Even in the lyrical sections there's a sort of uplift – an almost physical sense that something is rising.' To some, her words might evoke the virtuosic violin ascents in the first movement, or the dancing lines of the third. For Hahn, though, it is the 'disproportionately substantial' second movement that has become most interesting over the years. 'That is where everything grows,' she says. 'I took dance lessons when I was younger so I think that, for me, it's about how you exist in the space of the sound. If you're looking at a large, beautiful creation, how do you move through that space, and where do you go first?'

These are decisions she will make anew in her first ever performance with the Leipzig Gewandhaus Orchestra this summer – an orchestra with a strong sense of musical identity, and one that she has wanted to work with for some time. They will unite under the familiar baton of Andris Nelsons, who, she says, 'never tries to steer the ship completely, but is fully capable of steering the ship any which way, and that's a wonderful feeling. You can have a real conversation through the music and change as you go, depending on how it develops.' She is excited to have that conversation at the Proms where, no matter how many times she performs there, the enormous Hall always leaves her 'a bit in awe'.

Monday 25 August

12.30pm–c1.30pm & 3.30pm–c4.30pm
Royal Albert Hall ☀

● £10–£28 (plus booking fee')

CBEEBIES

CBeebies Prom: A Magical Bedtime Story

Sinfonia Smith Square
Ellie Slorach conductor

There will be no interval

AD *Audio-described by Timna Fibert*
BSL *British Sign Language-interpreted by Angie Newman*

Join CBeebies friends and a special guest in the *Bedtime Stories* chair as they share an enchanting musical tale. Don't miss this entertaining introduction to the orchestra for little ones – full of fun and laughs for all the family!

These are relaxed performances, designed to suit individuals or groups who feel more comfortable attending concerts in an informal environment. There is a relaxed attitude to noise and audience members are free to leave and re-enter the auditorium at any point. Chill-out areas offer a space for anyone who needs some quiet time before or during the performance. For full details, visit bbc.co.uk/proms.

🖥 *Broadcast on CBeebies and BBC iPlayer*

Every Prom is broadcast on BBC Radio 3 and BBC Sounds

Tuesday 26 August

7.30pm–c9.45pm • Royal Albert Hall

● £33–£110 (plus booking fee')

ANDRIS NELSONS

Sibelius's Second

Arvo Pärt Cantus in memoriam Benjamin Britten   6'
Dvořák Violin Concerto in A minor 32'

INTERVAL

Sibelius Symphony No. 2 in D major   46'

Hilary Hahn violin

Leipzig Gewandhaus Orchestra
Andris Nelsons conductor

The prestigious Leipzig Gewandhaus Orchestra – the world's longest-established symphony orchestra, famous for the glossy richness of its 'Leipzig sound' – returns to the Proms under Music Director Andris Nelsons. Joining them, and back at the Proms for the first time since 2010, is American violinist Hilary Hahn, soloist in Dvořák's colourful, folk-inspired Violin Concerto. The elemental power of Sibelius's Symphony No. 2, with its heroic final movement, has become indelibly associated with Finland's fight for freedom, no less personal a statement than the fragile, hypnotic beauty of Arvo Pärt's tribute to Benjamin Britten. *See pages 38–41.*

Wednesday 27 August

6.30pm–c10.05pm • Royal Albert Hall

● £26–£86 *(plus booking fee')*

HUW MONTAGUE RENDALL

'The Marriage of Figaro' from Glyndebourne

Mozart The Marriage of Figaro *170'*
(semi-staged; sung in Italian, with English surtitles)

Cast to include:

Tommaso Barea *Figaro*
Huw Montague Rendall *Count*
Louise Alder *Countess*
Johanna Wallroth *Susanna*
Alessandro Corbelli *Bartolo*
Madeleine Shaw *Marcellina*
Adèle Charvet *Cherubino*
Elisabeth Boudreault *Barbarina*
Alexander Vassiliev *Antonio*
Vincent Ordonneau *Don Curzio*

Glyndebourne Festival Opera
Orchestra of the Age of Enlightenment
Riccardo Minasi *conductor*
Talia Stern *stage director*

There will be one interval

Love conquers all … doesn't it? Mozart's sexiest and sharpest comedy pits men against women and master against servant as it cuts to the heart of human nature. Cherubino pines for the Countess, who is devoted to the Count. But he has designs on Susanna, who only has eyes for Figaro. Mozart's masterpiece of tangled desires, politics and identities comes fresh from the Glyndebourne Festival in the concert-staging of a brand-new production with a stellar cast, conducted by Riccardo Minasi.

Thursday 28 August

7.30pm–c9.35pm • Royal Albert Hall

◐ £11–£56 *(plus booking fee')*

INMO YANG

Saint-Saëns's 'Organ' Symphony

Bizet L'Arlésienne – Suite No. 1 *17'*
Sarasate Carmen Fantasy *12'*

INTERVAL

Holmès Andromède *15'*
Saint-Saëns Symphony No. 3 in C minor, 'Organ' *36'*

Inmo Yang *violin*
Rachel Mahon *organ*

BBC Symphony Orchestra
Marie Jacquot *conductor*

An all-French programme whose first half celebrates the bright, exotic colours conjured by Bizet, who died 150 years ago. As well as a suite from his incidental music for 'The Girl from Arles', we hear the fantasy for violin and orchestra featuring music – including the famous 'Habanera' – from his best-loved opera, reimagined with explosive virtuosity by Sarasate. South Korean violinist Inmo Yang makes his Proms debut in the seductive, mercurial mantle of Bizet's Gypsy-heroine. Saint-Saëns's spectacular Symphony No. 3 puts the 9,999 pipes of the Royal Albert Hall organ (nicknamed the 'Voice of Jupiter') in the spotlight at the climax of this monumental work, and there's more musical drama from gods and sea monsters in Augusta Holmès's tone-poem *Andromède*.

Spotlight on …

Marie Jacquot • 28 August

As a child, Marie Jacquot did not like classical music. She wanted to play tennis, not conduct – until, that is, she played trombone in her first orchestral performance, of the first suite from Bizet's *L'Arlésienne*. 'From that moment the joy of music grew inside me,' she says. 'It's probably because of that Bizet that I became a musician.'

That piece, then, makes a meaningful start to Jacquot's Proms – and UK – debut. She is excited, she says, to go even 'faster and deeper into the music'. That will be important from the resolute beginning of the Bizet, through the drama of the Sarasate, to the romantic, Wagnerian Holmès. Most of all, though, she will treasure her exploration of the Saint-Saëns. 'For me, the second movement is like a prayer to everybody I have liked who has passed away,' she says. Once, when she asked an orchestra to play it for those they had loved and lost, she nearly reduced the players to tears. Their sad thoughts were chased away only by subsequent cheerful blasts from the brass.

Would she like to jump from the podium in this happier moment, to join in on her trombone? 'Oh, yes, absolutely!' she laughs. To end, part of her hopes that – as in her favourite online video, of Tchaikovsky's Symphony No. 4 conducted by Gennady Rozhdestvensky at the Proms in 1971 – the audience will burst into applause partway through the last note.

Spotlight on ...
Khatia Buniatishvili
29 August

Khatia Buniatishvili first performed Tchaikovsky's Piano Concerto No. 1 when she was 17 – one of her earliest memories of playing with a full symphony orchestra. It was an incredible feeling, she says. It gives her fond memories of the music and has imprinted something of it in her genes. 'There are certain pieces that follow you through life, but even as your perceptions change, their essence stays the same,' she says. 'Human brains want something more beautiful, more fairy-tale-like, than just everyday reality. Tchaikovsky can take us there, in an imaginative and human way.'

That this concerto is so well loved and often performed does not intimidate Buniatishvili. Rather, it prompts the curiosity and daring to find her own way. 'What has already been defined can be redefined,' she says. 'It's like a wave: there is no precise shape of it, but the energy is there and that is what counts the most.' In this Prom she is eager to harness that energy in a new collaboration with the Melbourne SO – 'though if it doesn't go well, we will never do it again!' she jokes. 'But that's what's special about this piece. I've played it in different places and with different people, and somehow we always find home. It doesn't matter where you are from. If you can find the common rhythm and breath of Tchaikovsky, and the sense of phrasing and dramaturgy, then really nothing matters anymore. It becomes Tchaikovsky, and we become one.'

Friday 29 August

7.30pm–c9.55pm • Royal Albert Hall

● £15–£66 (plus booking fee*)

JAIME MARTÍN

Khatia Buniatishvili Plays Tchaikovsky

M. Sutherland Haunted Hills   15'

Tchaikovsky Piano Concerto No. 1 in B flat minor   35'

INTERVAL

Dvořák Symphony No. 6 in D major   43'

Khatia Buniatishvili *piano*

Melbourne Symphony Orchestra
Jaime Martín *conductor*

The Melbourne Symphony Orchestra returns to the Proms for the first time in 11 years, under Chief Conductor Jaime Martín, bringing two Romantic orchestral classics as well as a musical postcard from Down Under. Dvořák swells simple folk melodies into sweeping orchestral statements in his Symphony No. 6, inspired by his Bohemian homeland and landscape, while Australia's 'haunted hills' are the starting point for Margaret Sutherland's evocative symphonic portrait of her nation's first Aboriginal inhabitants. Former BBC Radio 3 New Generation Artist Khatia Buniatishvili is the soloist in Tchaikovsky's beloved Piano Concerto No. 1, with its passionate opening and the melting lilt of its slow movement.

Saturday 30 August

11am–c1.05pm • Royal Albert Hall ☀

● £26–£86 (plus booking fee*)

PETER MOORE

Rattle Conducts Folk Songs and Dances

Vaughan Williams English Folk Song Suite   14'

Schuller Eine kleine Posaunenmusik   16'

INTERVAL

Tippett Triumph: A paraphrase on music from 'The Mask of Time'   15'

Arnold English Dances, Set No. 1 (version for wind band)   9'

Grainger
The Lads of Wamphray   9'
Country Gardens   6'
A Lincolnshire Posy   16'

Peter Moore *trombone*

London Symphony Orchestra (wind, brass and percussion)
Sir Simon Rattle *conductor*

Sir Simon Rattle is back for a reunion with the London Symphony Orchestra, whose wind, brass and percussion celebrate the brilliant colours of folk-song arrangements by Vaughan Williams, Grainger and Arnold. They also perform Gunther Schuller's eclectic trombone concerto *Eine kleine Posaunenmusik*, with its hints of jazz and daring technical demands. The LSO's former Principal Trombone Peter Moore is the soloist.

Saturday 30 August

7.30pm–c9.55pm • Royal Albert Hall

● £11–£56 *(plus booking fee')*

HILARY CRONIN

Handel's 'Alexander's Feast'

Handel Alexander's Feast
(1742 version)   107'
(sung in English)

Hilary Cronin *soprano*
Hugh Cutting *counter-tenor*
Stuart Jackson *tenor*

Irish Baroque Chorus
Irish Baroque Orchestra
Peter Whelan *conductor*

There will be one interval

Award-winning Baroque dynamos Peter Whelan and the Irish Baroque Orchestra, praised for their 'stylish verve' and 'rich insight and charisma', make their Proms debut with a Handel rarity that celebrates the power of music itself. *Alexander's Feast* is an oratorio of operatic intensity, setting John Dryden's poem about the musician Timotheus, who stirs Alexander the Great to destructive revenge. The piece is heard for the first time at the Proms in the three-part version the composer made for performances in Dublin in 1742. *See page 72.*

Sunday 31 August

7.30pm–c9.40pm • Royal Albert Hall

● £15–£66 *(plus booking fee')*

PEKKA KUUSISTO

Pekka Kuusisto and Katarina Barruk

Songs by Katarina Barruk (based on the joik indigenous song-type from Sábmie) – interspersed with music by J. S. Bach, Philip Glass, Hannah Kendall (UK premiere), Caroline Shaw and Tippett   c50'

INTERVAL

Arvo Pärt Fratres   9'
Shostakovich, arr. Barshai
Chamber Symphony in C minor
(String Quartet No. 8)   24'

Katarina Barruk *vocals*
Arnljot Nordvik *guitar*
Christer Jørgensen *drums*

Norwegian Chamber Orchestra
Pekka Kuusisto *violin/director*

Pekka Kuusisto brings the strings of his Norwegian Chamber Orchestra to the Proms for a programme that reflects on human injustice. Shostakovich wrote his String Quartet No. 8 in Dresden, contemplating the Allied bombing of the city during the Second World War. For some, the work also speaks of the oppression of the Russian people under Stalin's rule. In a different time and place, singer and composer Katarina Barruk – one of only a handful of remaining speakers of the Ume Sámi language – is a living beacon for her native tongue and culture, performing songs that combine the traditional and the modern. *See pages 38–41, 58–62.*

Spotlight on ...

Peter Whelan • 30 August

AUG | 31 AUG

At school in 1980s Dublin, Peter Whelan remembers, 'We had a little history book with a section about how Handel performed in Dublin's Fishamble Street, with a drawing of him in a big wig. I was fascinated.' As an adult he decided to find out more. Handel had enjoyed visiting Ireland in 1741, he discovered, and had successfully premiered *Messiah* there in 1742. But by then he had fallen out of favour with Jonathan Swift, the author of *Gulliver's Travels*, Dean of St Patrick's Cathedral and, most importantly, the source of Handel's singers. Handel had to instead use local theatre musicians for a forthcoming performance of *Alexander's Feast*, rewriting it to accommodate them.

This Prom marks the culmination of Whelan and his colleagues' research into that 1742 performance. It is in three parts, rather than two, with solos reassigned and an extra aria reconstructed using the 'Dublin' libretto and a bass-line found at London's Royal College of Music. 'It's been amazing to reconnect it with Dublin and the musicians in the city at that time. It brings it to life in a different way.' To ensure every note is heard, the Irish Baroque Orchestra has invited back almost everyone it's ever worked with. 'It will be the biggest our orchestra has ever been,' says Whelan, 'like a giant party version of itself. We've been through such a journey discovering this music together, so it will feel like a huge celebration.'

Spotlight on ...
Amanda Majeski
1 September

For a singer used to performing Handel and Mozart, *The Lady Macbeth of the Mtsensk District* is no gentle introduction to Shostakovich. Nevertheless, the role of Katerina in this Prom will be Amanda Majeski's Shostakovich debut. 'There's no lightness in it, I'll say!' she laughs. 'The writing is an interesting mix of lyricism and brutality. There's this cacophony of male voices that uses such vulgar, derogatory words towards Katerina. She is a victim of a really oppressive society. The way that she stands up for herself, and for all women, is fascinating to me.'

Does this make Katerina's behaviour, as a triple murderess, justifiable to her? 'When you play a character, you have to empathise with them, even if they make choices that you would not make,' she says. 'It's my job to tell Katerina's story as truthfully as I can, and then let the audience form their own opinion. I hope it will provoke them and make them think: what would you do in that situation? Would you blow up, or would you stand quietly in the corner?'

Will this brutal role have a psychological impact on Majeski beyond the stage? She hopes not. 'I've done some pretty brutal roles before, like in Weinberg's *The Passenger*, and sometimes in rehearsals you do get emotional, you do let it get to you a little bit,' she says. 'But ultimately you let that feeling release through you and towards the audience. I think it's the only way to keep your sanity.'

Monday 1 September

6.30pm–*c*9.45pm • Royal Albert Hall

● £15–£66 *(plus booking fee')*

BRINDLEY SHERRATT

Shostakovich's 'Lady Macbeth'

Shostakovich The Lady Macbeth of the Mtsensk District *160'*
(semi-staged; sung in English, with English surtitles)

Amanda Majeski *Katerina*
Brindley Sherratt *Boris/Ghost of Boris*
John Findon *Zinovy*
Thomas Mole *Mill-hand/Priest*
Nicky Spence *Sergey*
Ava Dodd *Aksinya/Convict*
Ronald Samm *Shabby Peasant*
Siphe Kwani *Steward*
Chuma Sijeqa *Police Sergeant*
William Morgan *Teacher*
Sir Willard White *Old Convict*
Niamh O'Sullivan *Sonyetka*

BBC Singers
Chorus of English National Opera
BBC Philharmonic Orchestra
John Storgårds *conductor*

There will be one interval

In Shostakovich's anniversary year, a chance to hear his blistering operatic tragedy with an 'innocent murderess' at its heart. Amanda Majeski stars as Katerina – the defiant Lady Macbeth – with tenor Nicky Spence as her lover Sergey and Brindley Sherratt as the brutal patriarch Boris. *See pages 58–62, 82–84.*

Tuesday 2 September

7.30pm–*c*9.35pm • Royal Albert Hall

● £10–£46 *(plus booking fee')*

THOMAS ADÈS

Adès Conducts the BBC SO

Sibelius The Swan of Tuonela *10'*
Gabriella Smith Breathing Forests *28'*
UK premiere

INTERVAL

Thomas Adès Five Spells from The Tempest *22'*
Sibelius The Tempest – Suite No. 1 *19'*

James McVinnie *organ*

BBC Symphony Orchestra
Thomas Adès *conductor*

Composer and conductor Thomas Adès has long been a fan of Sibelius: 'He's obsessed with nature – you've always got this sense that he is on the edge of some vast wilderness.' Adès drew inspiration from the Finnish composer's incidental music for *The Tempest* when writing his own opera on the Shakespeare play. He conducts suites from both these storm-laden, supernatural works, along with *The Swan of Tuonela*, in which Sibelius summoned up his skill as a bard of Swedish folk tales. James McVinnie is the soloist in Gabriella Smith's organ concerto *Breathing Forests*, a cavernous 'sonic forest' and howl of protest against natural destruction.

Wednesday 3 September

8pm–c9.30pm • Royal Albert Hall

● £15–£66 (plus booking fee')

ST. VINCENT

St. Vincent at the BBC Proms

St. Vincent

Jules Buckley Orchestra
Jules Buckley conductor

There will be no interval

She's the queen of 'raw emotion, electrifying rock and unrestrained self-expression'. Now, fresh from three 2025 Grammy wins – including Best Rock Song and Best Alternative Music Album – St. Vincent makes her BBC Proms debut in a unique UK performance. Widely regarded as one of the most innovative and fascinating artists in modern music, the chart-topping American 'art-rock siren' collaborates with Jules Buckley and his orchestra, performing brand-new symphonic arrangements of tracks from her eclectic back catalogue.

£8 Promming tickets available for every concert

Thursday 4 September

7.30pm–c9.45pm • Royal Albert Hall

● £15–£66 (plus booking fee')

EDWIN OUTWATER

Classic Thriller Soundtracks

Programme to include excerpts from:

Herrmann
Vertigo
Psycho
North by Northwest
Taxi Driver

and music from film scores by Quincy Jones, David Raksin and Miklós Rózsa

BBC Concert Orchestra
Edwin Outwater conductor

There will be one interval

From the shrieking strings of *Psycho* to the brooding jazz-club sleaze of *Taxi Driver*: Bernard Herrmann's music is the soundtrack to the greats of Hollywood's Golden Age. Join the BBC Concert Orchestra and its Principal Guest Conductor and Curator Edwin Outwater to celebrate the composer's iconic film scores: A programme rich with suspense and drama also includes music by Herrmann's celebrated Hollywood colleagues. *See pages 100–102.*

🖵 *Broadcast on BBC Four and BBC iPlayer this season*

Friday 5 September

7.30pm–c9.30pm • Royal Albert Hall

● £15–£66 (plus booking fee')

SIR SIMON RATTLE

Rattle Conducts Chineke!

S. Coleridge-Taylor
The Bamboula   10'

Walker Sinfonia No. 5, 'Visions'   17'

INTERVAL

Shostakovich Symphony No. 10
in E minor   57'

Chineke! Orchestra
Sir Simon Rattle conductor

Experience the 'electric atmosphere' of a performance by the Chineke! Orchestra – Europe's first minority Black and ethnically diverse orchestra – conducted for the first time by Sir Simon Rattle. Together they perform Shostakovich's 10th Symphony: over 50 minutes of brutality, violence, despair and terror, followed by two minutes of defiance. A portrait of life – and death – in Stalin's Russia, it's a fierce act of musical testimony. Bearing witness is also central to Pulitzer-winner George Walker's Sinfonia No. 5, a work 'suffused with anger', raging against the 2015 Charleston church massacre. The Prom opens with the steady thrum of Coleridge-Taylor's orchestral dance *The Bamboula. See pages 58–62.*

🖵 *Broadcast on BBC Four and BBC iPlayer this season*

Saturday 6 September

7.30pm–c10.05pm • Royal Albert Hall

● £15–£66 *(plus booking fee*)*

GOLDA SCHULTZ

Golda Schultz Sings Gershwin and Bernstein

Programme to include:

Schreker Chamber Symphony   28'

Stravinsky The Firebird – suite (1945 version)   28'

and songs/arias from:

Bernstein West Side Story

Gershwin Porgy and Bess

Korngold Die tote Stadt

Stravinsky The Rake's Progress

Weill Lost in the Stars

Golda Schultz *soprano*

Chamber Orchestra of Europe
Robin Ticciati *conductor*

South African soprano Golda Schultz, the 'glorious' star of 2020's Last Night, returns to the Proms with songs by Bernstein, Gershwin, Weill and others. Bask in the sultry heat of the Deep South in 'Summertime' from *Porgy and Bess*; feel the intensity of first love in 'Somewhere' from *West Side Story*. A programme of contrasting moods and colours also includes Schreker's sensuous Chamber Symphony – glittering and mercurial – and the bold, folk-infused dances of Stravinsky's ballet *The Firebird*.

Sunday 7 September

11am–c1.10pm • Royal Albert Hall ☀

● £15–£66 *(plus booking fee*)*

ARABELLA STEINBACHER

Vaughan Williams's 'A London Symphony'

Respighi Pines of Rome   23'

Milhaud Le boeuf sur le toit (version for violin and orchestra)   19'

INTERVAL

Vaughan Williams Symphony No. 2 (A London Symphony)   44'

Arabella Steinbacher *violin*

Royal Philharmonic Orchestra
Vasily Petrenko *conductor*

Rome, Paris, London: Vasily Petrenko and the Royal Philharmonic Orchestra take us on a musical tour of Europe. Children play in the gardens of Rome's Villa Borghese, and a nightingale sings at night in high branches on the Janiculum Hill: Respighi's colourful outdoor portrait of Italy's capital contrasts with both the smoky thrum and after-hours jazz rhythms of Milhaud's *Le boeuf sur le toit* – a musical homage to Paris – and the impressionistic colours of Vaughan Williams's *A London Symphony*, in which Big Ben's chimes and a busker's harmonica break through the urban bustle.

Sunday 7 September

7.30pm–c9.45pm • Royal Albert Hall

● £11–£56 *(plus booking fee*)*

ELIZABETH WATTS

Grieg's Piano Concerto

Gipps Death on the Pale Horse   8'

Grieg Piano Concerto in A minor   30'

INTERVAL

Bliss The Beatitudes   50'

Elizabeth Watts *soprano*
Laurence Kilsby *tenor*
Lukas Sternath *piano*

BBC Singers
BBC Symphony Chorus
BBC Symphony Orchestra
Sakari Oramo *conductor*

Prize-winning young Viennese pianist Lukas Sternath makes his Proms debut in Grieg's beloved Piano Concerto, with its heart-on-sleeve melodies and intimate lyricism. The piece is framed by two musical products of war: a haunting elegy by Vaughan Williams's pupil Ruth Gipps, inspired by a William Blake illustration of the Four Horsemen of the Apocalypse, and anniversary-composer Arthur Bliss's *The Beatitudes*, a cantata composed for the reopening in 1962 of Coventry Cathedral – part Passion, part howl of human loss, part musical prayer for a 'troubled world'.

Monday 8 September

7.30pm–c9.45pm • Royal Albert Hall

● **£26–£86** (plus booking fee*)

FRANZ WELSER-MÖST

Vienna Philharmonic Plays Bruckner's Ninth

Berg Lulu Suite   32'

INTERVAL

Bruckner Symphony No. 9
in D minor   63'

Vienna Philharmonic
Franz Welser-Möst *conductor*

One of the world's great orchestras, the Vienna Philharmonic concludes this year's triptych of ninth symphonies with the grandest of them all. Dedicated to God, Bruckner's Symphony No. 9 is the extraordinary product of a career's experience and a decade's labour – an unfinished swansong that confronts darkness even as it grasps towards heaven in music the composer himself thought 'the most beautiful I have ever written'. The concert opens with Berg's *Lulu Suite*, a distillation of the composer's tragic opera into a heady and sometimes violent outpouring for orchestra. *See pages 78–81.*

Every Prom is broadcast on BBC Radio 3 and BBC Sounds

Tuesday 9 September

6.30pm–c8.25pm • Royal Albert Hall

● **£33–£110** (plus booking fee*)

FRANZ WELSER-MÖST

Vienna Philharmonic Plays Mozart and Tchaikovsky

Mozart Symphony No. 38
in D major, 'Prague'   29'

INTERVAL

Tchaikovsky Symphony No. 6
in B minor, 'Pathétique'   50'

Vienna Philharmonic
Franz Welser-Möst *conductor*

Franz Welser-Möst and the Vienna Philharmonic round off their Proms visits with two late, great symphonies, each breaking the musical mould. Hot on the heels of *The Marriage of Figaro*, Mozart's 'Prague' Symphony is animated by the same iconoclastic brilliance, bewitching audiences with a thematic richness, breadth and ambition that outpaced any previous symphony. A century later it was Tchaikovsky's turn to defy convention with his final, 'Pathétique' Symphony – whose confessional intensity and turbulent passions conceal a secret narrative known only to the composer. Huge melodies soar and surge, but there's no happy ending; the symphony closes not with a shout of triumph but with a heart-breaking lament.

🖵 Broadcast on BBC Four and BBC iPlayer this season

Tuesday 9 September

10.15pm–c11.30pm • Royal Albert Hall 🌙

◐ **£10–£28** (plus booking fee*)

Late Night

AVI AVITAL

Avi Avital: Between Worlds

Ensemble Rustavi
Between Worlds Ensemble
Avi Avital *mandolin/director*

Bordering Bulgaria, Georgia, Romania, Russia, Turkey and Ukraine, the Black Sea is a musical crossroads – a junction between worlds. Join boundary-breaking mandolin virtuoso Avi Avital – making his Proms debut – his Between Worlds Ensemble and Georgia's male-voice Ensemble Rustavi for a sonic tour of these vibrant neighbouring cultures that includes traditional Crimean Tatar music, Turkish folk and klezmer, as well as works by Bartók and Fazil Say.

£8 Promming tickets available for every concert

Spotlight on ...
Delyana Lazarova
10 September

10
SEP
|
13
SEP

'I'm already dreaming about this programme,' says Delyana Lazarova of her Proms debut. She's performed at the Royal Albert Hall before, as Assistant Conductor to Sir Mark Elder and the Hallé, and it's an experience she's keen to relive with Anastasia Kobekina and the BBC Scottish Symphony Orchestra. 'We have this wonderful energy between us,' she says of Kobekina. 'And with the BBC SSO, from just a few minutes into our first rehearsal I felt the chemistry. Musically it was so easy: it was as if the sky was the limit.'

The pieces in this Prom are special too, Lazarova feels, because each creates 'a symphonic painting that is absolutely timeless. The colours, transparency and depth of Boulanger's orchestration are incredible. It's as though you open the window on a spring morning – everything is fresh and beautiful.' The Shostakovich, coloured by the bleakness of Stalin's Russia, 'takes us to the darkest type of human experience, with so much strength. It's as relevant now as it was when he wrote it.' Lazarova refuses to cut any of Rachmaninov's hour-long Symphony No. 2, as some do. Though he agreed to make cuts, she says, 'each time, he said it felt like they cut out part of his heart. His music is so evocative, so full of warmth and beauty, with Romanticism and melodic lushness on the highest level. I want to give time for it to develop as he wanted, to tell his story in all its detail.'

Wednesday 10 September
7.30pm–c9.50pm • Royal Albert Hall

● £11–£56 *(plus booking fee')*

ANASTASIA KOBEKINA

Rachmaninov's Second Symphony

L. Boulanger D'un matin de printemps 5'

Shostakovich Cello Concerto No. 1 in E flat major 30'

INTERVAL

Rachmaninov Symphony No. 2 in E minor 60'

Anastasia Kobekina *cello*

BBC Scottish Symphony Orchestra
Delyana Lazarova *conductor*

The ultimate Romantic symphony, Rachmaninov's Second has it all: heartfelt emotions, endless melodies, a slow movement whose two rival themes eventually find themselves locked in a passionate embrace and a radiant finale. The BBC Scottish Symphony Orchestra and Principal Guest Conductor Designate Delyana Lazarova are joined by former BBC Radio 3 New Generation Artist and 'unrivalled musician' Anastasia Kobekina for Shostakovich's supremely demanding Cello Concerto No. 1. The Prom opens with dawn breaking on a spring morning in Lili Boulanger's vivid tone-poem *D'un matin de printemps*. *See pages 58–62.*

Thursday 11 September
7.30pm–c9.25pm • Royal Albert Hall

● £10–£46 *(plus booking fee')*

ILAN VOLKOV

Brahms's Second Symphony

Gabrieli, ed. Maderna In ecclesiis 10'
Stravinsky Requiem Canticles 15'

INTERVAL

Gabrieli, ed. Maderna Canzone a tre cori 5'

Brahms Symphony No. 2 in D major 45'

Jess Dandy *contralto*
Ashley Riches *bass-baritone*

National Youth Choir
BBC Scottish Symphony Orchestra
Ilan Volkov *conductor*

Solemn ritual and holiday sunshine collide in a concert by Ilan Volkov and the BBC Scottish Symphony Orchestra. The incense-scented processional splendour of Gabrieli's *In ecclesiis* and *Canzone a tre core*, transcribed with contemporary clarity by Bruno Maderna, frame Stravinsky's last major work – the 'pocket-requiem' he knew he was 'writing for himself'. Step out of church and into the pastoral warmth of Brahms's happiest symphony, written on the slopes of the Austrian Alps: 'all blue sky, babbling streams, sunshine and cool green shade'.

Friday 12 September

7.30pm–c10.05pm • Royal Albert Hall

● **£15–£66** (plus booking fee*)

JOHN WILSON

John Wilson Conducts Bernstein and Ravel

R. Strauss Don Juan   20'
Bernstein Serenade   30'

INTERVAL

Ravel Daphnis and Chloe   58'

James Ehnes violin

Sinfonia of London Chorus
Sinfonia of London
John Wilson conductor

Critics have praised their Proms performances as 'breathtaking', 'blazing' and 'simply as good as it gets'. Now John Wilson and the Sinfonia of London double down with a passion-soaked programme of 20th-century orchestral showpieces. Love is the theme of a Prom that opens with history's greatest seducer, Don Juan, in Strauss's swashbuckling tone-poem, and closes with the sensuous, diaphanous textures of Ravel's ballet *Daphnis and Chloe*. At the centre is one of Bernstein's most lyrical orchestral works. James Ehnes is the soloist in *Serenade* – a violin concerto by another name that muses on, and interrogates, the nature of love itself. *See pages 22–26.*

Saturday 13 September

7pm–10.30pm • Royal Albert Hall

○ **£50–£160** (plus booking fee*)

ELIM CHAN

Last Night of the Proms 2025

Programme to include:

Mussorgsky A Night on the Bare Mountain (original version, 1867)   12'

Hummel Trumpet Concerto
in E major   19'

A. Benjamin, arr. **Herrmann** Storm Cloud Cantata (from 'The Man Who Knew too Much')   12'

Lehár The Merry Widow –
Vilja Song   5'

Gounod Faust – 'Ah, je ris de me voir' (Jewel Song)   7'

Camille Pépin Fireworks   c6'
BBC commission: world premiere

Dukas The Sorcerer's Apprentice   12'

Shostakovich Festive Overture   7'

Rachel Portman Gatherings   c3'
BBC commission: world premiere

arr. Wood Fantasia on British Sea-Songs   13'

Arne, arr. **Sargent** Rule, Britannia!   3'

Elgar Pomp and Circumstance March No. 1 in D major ('Land of Hope and Glory')   8'

LOUISE ALDER

Parry, orch. **Elgar** Jerusalem   2'
arr. Britten The National Anthem   2'
Trad., arr. **P. Campbell**
Auld lang syne   2'

Louise Alder soprano
Alison Balsom trumpet

BBC Singers
BBC Symphony Chorus
BBC Symphony Orchestra
Elim Chan conductor

There will be one interval

The biggest night in classical music is back! After eight weeks and over 80 concerts, the 2025 BBC Proms celebrates with a Last Night spectacular, packed with musical surprises and star turns. Elim Chan conducts the BBC Symphony Orchestra and Chorus in all the traditional favourites – anthems, folk songs and singalongs – with solo performances by 'captivating' soprano Louise Alder and 'sensational' trumpeter Alison Balsom. There's a nod to this season's Bernard Herrmann celebration, a mischevous sorcerer's apprentice from Dukas, and premieres by Camille Pépin and Rachel Portman. *See pages 58–62, 100–102.*

🖥 *Broadcast live on BBC Two (first half),
BBC One (second half) and BBC iPlayer*

BBC.CO.UK/PROMS   **141**

Thursday 24 July

THE FIRE STATION, SUNDERLAND
8pm–c9.30pm

SOWETO KINCH

'Round Midnight with Soweto Kinch

Soweto Kinch *presenter*

There will be no interval

Soweto Kinch – jazz saxophonist, hip hop artist, curator and presenter – has developed an enviable presence on the UK music scene. Tonight he hosts a special edition in Sunderland of his acclaimed late-night Radio 3 show *'Round Midnight*, which celebrates the best in jazz from all eras and around the globe, with a particular focus on new UK artists. 'There's such a breadth and diversity of expression within what we call jazz,' says Kinch. So expect an eclectic mix of special guests and chat, steered by Kinch's guiding hand and propelled by his gift for drawing audiences into the orbit of his wide-ranging passions.

📻 *Recorded for future broadcast on BBC Radio 3*

Proms Gateshead

Friday 25 July

THE GLASSHOUSE INTERNATIONAL CENTRE FOR MUSIC
9.15pm–c10.45pm • Sage One 🌙

ROBERT AMES

Robert Ames and Royal Northern Sinfonia

Royal Northern Sinfonia
Robert Ames *conductor*

There will be no interval

Following on from the success of last year's poetic electro soul collaboration with Jordan Rakei and 2023's euphoric Prom with Self Esteem, the ever-eclectic conductor and arranger Robert Ames continues his explorations into new musical sound-worlds. Ames is no stranger to the Proms, where he has led previous ambitious events celebrating early electronic music, as well as soundtracks from video games and sci-fi films. *See bbc.co.uk/ proms for further details.*

Saturday 26 July

THE GLASSHOUSE INTERNATIONAL CENTRE FOR MUSIC
5.30pm–c7pm • Sage Two

ANGELINE MORRISON

Angeline Morrison: The Sorrow Songs (Folk Songs of Black British Experience)

Angeline Morrison

There will be no interval

Intimate, haunting and expressing the essence of traditional English folk song, Angeline Morrison's 2022 album *The Sorrow Songs: Folk Songs of Black British Experience* tells the untold stories of people from the African diaspora and their place in these islands. Here are musical tales of the 'Unknown African Boy (d.1830)', an enslaved child whose body was washed up on the Isles of Scilly; or 'Black John', the first known Black horticulturist in Britain; or 'The Beautiful Spotted Black Boy', an enslaved child born with vitiligo, whose patchy complexion caused him to be paraded as a curiosity. In researching and telling these stories, Morrison both preserves and reinvigorates the rich tapestry of English folk music. She performs here with The Sorrow Songs Band and a special guest.

Saturday 26 July

**THE GLASSHOUSE
INTERNATIONAL CENTRE FOR MUSIC**
7.30pm–c9.30pm • Sage One

DINIS SOUSA

Bach and Mendelssohn with Royal Northern Sinfonia

J. S. Bach Keyboard Concerto
in D minor, BWV 1052   22'

INTERVAL

Mendelssohn Symphony No. 2
in B flat major, 'Lobgesang'   63'

Julie Roset *soprano*
Adèle Charvet *mezzo-soprano*
Benjamin Hulett *tenor*
David Fray *piano*

Voices of the River's Edge
Chorus of Royal Northern Sinfonia
Huddersfield Choral Society

Royal Northern Sinfonia
Dinis Sousa *conductor*

Mendelssohn's Second Symphony is a
'Hymn of Praise', an expression of joy and
faith, replete with dances, fanfares and hymns.
The dark, sober beauty of Bach's Keyboard
Concerto in D minor offers a stark contrast.

⌨ *Broadcast on BBC Four and BBC iPlayer this season*

Sunday 27 July

**THE GLASSHOUSE
INTERNATIONAL CENTRE FOR MUSIC**
1.30pm–c2.45pm & 4pm–c5.15pm
Sage One ☀

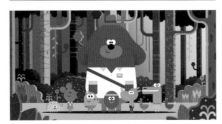

HEY DUGGEE

CBeebies Prom: Wildlife Jamboree

Royal Northern Sinfonia

There will be no interval

Join Duggee, Bluey, the Octonauts and lots
more of your CBeebies friends to celebrate
the natural world in music and song at the
spectacular Wildlife Jamboree. Joined by the
Royal Northern Sinfonia and your favourite
CBeebies presenters, there'll be plenty of
animal fun and maybe a wildlife muddle or
two! *See pages 52–55.*

Sunday 27 July

**THE GLASSHOUSE INTERNATIONAL
CENTRE FOR MUSIC**
3pm–c4.45pm • Sage Two ☀

SEAN SHIBE

Sean Shibe and Friends

Tyshawn Sorey new work   c10'
BBC co-commission

Cassandra Miller Bel canto   17'

INTERVAL

Boulez Le marteau sans maître 40'

Sean Shibe *guitars*
Ema Nikolovska *mezzo-soprano*
George Barton, Sam Wilson,
  Iris van den Bos *percussion*
Adam Walker *alto flute*
Ruth Chinyere Gibson *viola*
Matthew Hunt *clarinet*
Mira Benjamin *violin*
Colin Alexander *cello*
Alphonse Cemin *conductor*

Guitar dynamo Sean Shibe is joined by a
group of starry musical friends to continue
our Boulez centenary celebrations. Among
two works by living composers, we hear
Boulez's seminal *Le marteau sans maître*,
the modernist masterpiece that reinvented
20th-century music. *See pages 68–71.*

Friday 8 August

ULSTER HALL, BELFAST
9pm–c10.30pm ☾

SIMON ARMITAGE

100 Years of the Shipping Forecast

Ulster Orchestra
Chloé Van Soeterstède *conductor*

There will be no interval

Cromarty, Forth, Tyne … The Proms celebrates the centenary of the *Shipping Forecast*, heard daily on BBC Radio 4, a lifeline to all those at sea and a poetic salve for countless others on land. With presenters from Radio 4's Continuity team, music inspired by the oceans and the elements, and a new work by Poet Laureate Simon Armitage and his group LYR, this is an event that speaks to the heart of our island nation.

Proms Bristol

Friday 22 August

BRISTOL BEACON
6pm–c7.15pm • Beacon Hall

THE BREATH

Paraorchestra and The Breath

The Breath
  Ríoghnach Connolly *voice/flute/shruti*
  Stuart McCallum *guitars*

Paraorchestra
Charles Hazlewood *conductor*

There will be no interval

Following its Proms debut last year, the Paraorchestra returns for a unique collaboration. Award-winning duo The Breath – featuring guitarist Stuart McCallum and singer/instrumentalist Ríoghnach Connolly – is known for its understated take on ambient, folk and gentle psychedelia. Led by Artistic Director Charles Hazlewood, the Paraorchestra brings its fearless and holistic approach to large-scale music-making, working with composer Oliver Vibrans to translate The Breath's unique sound-world into an orchestral space – all combined with ethereal vocals for an other-worldly landscape.

Friday 22 August

BRISTOL BEACON
10pm–c11.30pm • Lantern Hall ☾

VERITY SHARP

Late Junction

Verity Sharp *presenter*

There will be no interval

From the music of after-hours Tokyo to Somalian disco, and from guest playlisters to the world's smallest LP, made for Queen Mary's dolls' house, Radio 3's *Late Junction* has been home to the adventurous listener for over 25 years. This special Proms edition welcomes guest artists who have forged distinctive musical paths, offering a late-night listening swerve that takes a sharp left off the beaten track.

Saturday 23 August

ST GEORGE'S BRISTOL
2pm–c3.15pm ☀

Danish National Vocal Ensemble

J. S. Bach Komm, Jesu, komm, BWV 229 — 8'

Ethel Smyth Five Sacred Partsongs – 'Komm, süsser Tod' — 5'

Palestrina Fratres ego enim accepi — 4'

Paola Prestini Fratres, after Palestrina — 7'

Carl Nielsen Three Motets — 15'

Anon. Three traditional Danish summer songs — 9'

Krek Three Autumn Songs — 8'

Mahler-Werfel, arr. C. Gottwald Five Songs – 'Laue Sommernacht' — 3'

Mahler, arr. N. Forte Rückert-Lieder – 'Liebst du um Schönheit' — 5'

Danish National Vocal Ensemble
Martina Batič *conductor*

There will be no interval

The Danish National Vocal Ensemble presents a choral dialogue across the centuries, with British composer and suffragette Ethel Smyth responding to Bach and Italian-born Paola Prestini reflecting on Palestrina, born 500 years ago. The great Dane Carl Nielsen paid his own tribute to Palestrina and the choir also brings songs of summer and autumn.

 *Recorded for future broadcast on BBC Radio 3*

Saturday 23 August

BRISTOL BEACON
5.30pm–c7.30pm • Beacon Hall

ZOË BEYERS

Mozart, Arvo Pärt and Gavin Higgins

Sibelius Rakastava — 11'

Arvo Pärt Tabula rasa — 30'

INTERVAL

Gavin Higgins Rough Voices* — 12'

Mozart Symphony No. 39 in E flat major — 28'

Zoë Beyers *violin/director*
Miranda Dale *violin*

Britten Sinfonia
*Tess Jackson *conductor*

Young love proclaims itself in Sibelius's ravishing *Rakastava*. Arvo Pärt's cult concerto for two violins *Tabula rasa* redefines sound, silence and the relationship between them, while Gavin Higgins's *Rough Voices* responds to the pandemic with a musical protest, giving voice to the most vulnerable. The first of Mozart's last three symphonies is part of a glittering final flourish in his career. *See pages 38–41.*

Sunday 24 August

BRISTOL BEACON
7pm–c9.15pm • Beacon Hall

AVERY AMEREAU

Under the Italian Sun

Rossini William Tell – overture — 12'

Puccini Capriccio sinfonico — 12'

Berio Folk Songs — 23'

INTERVAL

Verdi I vespri siciliani – overture — 9'

Respighi Il tramonto — 16'

Elgar In the South (Alassio) — 20'

Avery Amereau *mezzo-soprano*

Orchestra of Welsh National Opera
Carlo Rizzi *conductor*

Elgar's *In the South* captures the exhilarating feeling of an afternoon by the Ligurian coast. Sunset comes and goes for two young lovers in Respighi's *Il tramonto*, whose quiet tragedy echoes the tensions in the overture from Verdi's *Sicilian Vespers*. There's exhilarating energy from Rossini's *William Tell* overture, and a chance to glance ahead to the joys of *Tosca* and *La bohème* in Puccini's tune-filled *Capriccio sinfonico*. *See pages 68–71.*

Sunday 7 September

ST GEORGE'S HALL, BRADFORD
3pm–c4.30pm ☀

ANGELIQUE KIDJO

Angélique Kidjo:
African Symphony

Angélique Kidjo, arr. Derrick
Hodge African Symphony   *c80'*
UK premiere

Angélique Kidjo

BBC Philharmonic Orchestra
Chris Cameron *conductor*

There will be no interval

'I want to show the world the richness and beauty of African culture … and I feel music is the best vehicle to carry that message.' That mission has sustained the career of five-time Grammy Award-winner Angélique Kidjo for over four decades. Following her Proms debut back in 2019, the Benin-born 'queen of African music' returns for a showcase as part of Bradford 2025 UK City of Culture, paying tribute to her African heritage and taking in iconic tracks from legends such as Miriam Makeba, Fela Kuti, Hugh Masekela and Youssou N'Dour. 'I wanted to tell a story based on my personal experience and my musical background,' says Kidjo. 'I also wanted to speak of the struggles that artists encounter in the pursuit of their music.'

BBC Young Composer Workshops

BBC PROMS YOUNG COMPOSER WORKSHOP, 2024

The Glasshouse International Centre for Music, Gateshead
Saturday 26 July

Royal Albert Hall and Imperial College, London
Saturday 16 August

Bristol Beacon
Wednesday 23 August

Produced in collaboration with BBC Introducing, the BBC Young Composer workshops offer young music-makers the chance to meet and learn from experienced composers, songwriters and musicians in the industry. Through a range of activities, the workshops will help to develop their skills in creating their own original music.

BBC Young Composer creates opportunities and resources for 12- to 18-year-olds across the UK who make their own original music. It holds a nationwide competition every two years. Past winners include Kristina Arakelyan, Thomas Hewitt Jones, Grace-Evangeline Mason, Mark Simpson and Asteryth Sloane.

The initiative offers a wealth of composition resources for both teachers and young people, and was conceived with the hope of inspiring more young people to get creative with music and to consider a career in the music industry.

For further information and current opportunities, visit bbc.co.uk/youngcomposer

Booking at the Royal Albert Hall

Online
royalalberthall.com or
bbc.co.uk/promstickets

By phone
on 020 7070 4441*

9am–5pm, weekdays, plus:
Saturday 17 May: 9am–8pm
Sunday 18 May: 9am–5pm

In person
at the Royal Albert
Hall Box Office

9am–9pm, daily; please note: until
18 July, on days where there is no
evening performance at the Hall, the
Door 12 Box Office will close at 5pm

---

24 April
Create your
Proms Plan online

From 9am on Thursday 24 April,
go to bbc.co.uk/promstickets and
fill in your Proms Planner. You must
complete and submit your Plan by
11.59pm on Friday 16 May in order
to make a booking. Creating a Plan
does not by itself result in a booking.

15 May
Book your
Promming Passes

From 9am on Thursday 15 May,
book your Season and Weekend
Promming (standing) Passes for the
Royal Albert Hall. (These passes are
not bookable in the Proms Planner.)

16 May
Booking opens for
The Traitors, the Relaxed Prom
and the CBeebies Proms

From 9am on Friday 16 May, book your
tickets for The Traitors (26 July), the
Relaxed Prom (10 August) and CBeebies
Proms (25 August). (These tickets are
not bookable in the Proms Planner.)

17 May
General booking opens

From 9am on Saturday 17 May,
submit your Proms Plan or book online
via bbc.co.uk/promstickets, in person
or by phone. See bbc.co.uk/promstickets
for details of how to book.

TICKETS FOR CONCERTS IN OTHER VENUES

Tickets for concerts in Belfast, Bradford, Bristol, Gateshead and Sunderland will be available directly from each venue, not the Royal Albert Hall.
(These tickets are not bookable via the Proms Planner.) See pages 151–152 for details.

* CALL COSTS

Standard geographic charges from landlines and mobiles apply. All calls may be recorded and monitored for training and quality-control purposes.

Royal Albert Hall ticket prices

Seated tickets for all Proms at the Royal Albert Hall fall into one of nine price bands, indicated at the top of each concert listing on pages 110–141. Promming (standing) tickets are available on the day of each concert for just £8 (including booking fee). See opposite for details.

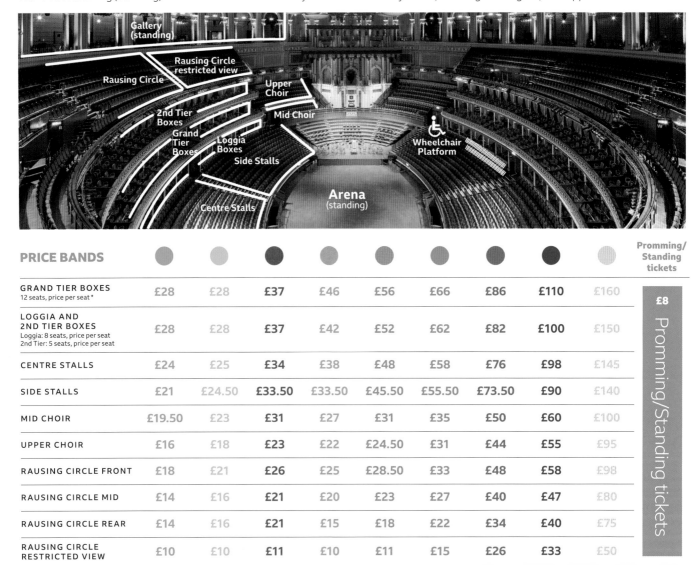

PRICE BANDS	●	●	●	●	●	●	●	●	●	Promming/ Standing tickets
GRAND TIER BOXES 12 seats, price per seat *	£28	£28	£37	£46	£56	£66	£86	£110	£160	£8
LOGGIA AND 2ND TIER BOXES Loggia: 8 seats, price per seat 2nd Tier: 5 seats, price per seat	£28	£28	£37	£42	£52	£62	£82	£100	£150	
CENTRE STALLS	£24	£25	£34	£38	£48	£58	£76	£98	£145	
SIDE STALLS	£21	£24.50	£33.50	£33.50	£45.50	£55.50	£73.50	£90	£140	
MID CHOIR	£19.50	£23	£31	£27	£31	£35	£50	£60	£100	
UPPER CHOIR	£16	£18	£23	£22	£24.50	£31	£44	£55	£95	
RAUSING CIRCLE FRONT	£18	£21	£26	£25	£28.50	£33	£48	£58	£98	
RAUSING CIRCLE MID	£14	£16	£21	£20	£23	£27	£40	£47	£80	
RAUSING CIRCLE REAR	£14	£16	£21	£15	£18	£22	£34	£40	£75	
RAUSING CIRCLE RESTRICTED VIEW	£10	£10	£11	£10	£11	£15	£26	£33	£50	

Promming/Standing tickets

Booking fees: a booking fee of 2% of the total value – plus £2 per ticket (£1 per ticket for the Relaxed Prom) up to a maximum of £25 – applies to all bookings (including Season and Weekend Promming Passes), other than those made in person at the Royal Albert Hall. Promming tickets cost £8; no additional booking fees apply, whether they are bought online or in person. An optional £1.50 per ticket levy will be added to tickets for Proms at the Royal Albert Hall.
*As most Grand Tier Boxes are privately owned, availability is limited.

There's a Prom for every music-lover, whether you're a first-timer or a seasoned regular. For the season calendar, see the inside back cover. Seats start from just £10 (plus booking fee) – and you can Prom (stand) for only £8 (including booking fee).

If you cannot use your ticket

Tickets cannot be refunded or exchanged after purchase. But, if you cannot use a ticket for any reason and want to try to resell it, we recommend using Twickets – an ethical ticket resale marketplace, enabling concert-goers to sell tickets at no more than face value.

Promming on the day

The popular tradition of Promming (standing in the Arena or Gallery areas of the Royal Albert Hall) is central to the unique atmosphere of the BBC Proms. Around 1,000 standing places in the Arena and Gallery are available on the day of each concert for just £8 (including booking fee). You can book up to two tickets online from 9.30am on the day of the concert. If you are unable to book online, you may be able to book in person at Door 12 of the Royal Albert Hall, subject to availability. Visit bbc.co.uk/proms for details.

Save money by buying a Season Promming Pass for £272. These offer priority access to standing places in the Arena or Gallery throughout the season (excluding the CBeebies, From Dark Till Dawn and Relaxed Proms, and a second performance of repeated Proms) plus savings on individual ticket prices, as well as guaranteed admission to the Last Night of the Proms. You can also save money by buying a Weekend Promming Pass. Please visit bbc.co.uk/proms for full details.

For information on Promming tickets for non-Royal Albert Hall concerts, see bbc.co.uk/promstickets.

A limited number of seats either at the back of the Arena or in the Choir or Gallery are available for those Prommers who are unable to stand for an entire concert. These seats can be booked online. See bbc.co.uk/proms for details.

Online booking

The 'Select Your Own Seat' option is not available via the Proms Planner or during the first few days that Proms tickets are on sale. You will be allocated the best available places within your chosen seating area. During this time is not possible to book an entire box online. If you would like to book a complete box, call the Box Office on 020 7070 4441.

18s and under go half-price

Tickets for people aged 18 and under can be purchased at half-price in any seating area of the Royal Albert Hall except for the Last Night. (Not applicable to Promming tickets.)

Great savings for groups

Groups of 10 or more attending Royal Albert Hall concerts can claim a 5% discount on the price of selected tickets (not including the Last Night). For details, call the Group Booking Information Line on 020 7070 4408.

Concerts across the UK

For information regarding tickets for non-Royal Albert Hall concerts, see bbc.co.uk/promstickets.

Last Night of the Proms

Owing to high demand, the majority of seated tickets for the Last Night of the Proms are allocated by ballot, as follows:

The Five-Concert Ballot

Customers who purchase tickets for at least five other concerts at the Royal Albert Hall are eligible to enter the Five-Concert Ballot. For details on how to enter, see bbc.co.uk/promstickets. The Five-Concert Ballot closes at midnight on Thursday 5 June.

If you require a wheelchair space for the Last Night, you will still need to book for five other concerts, but you must phone the Access Information Line (020 7070 4410) before 5pm on Thursday 5 June to enter the separate ballot for wheelchair spaces.

The Open Ballot

One hundred Centre Stalls seats (priced £145 each, plus booking fee) and 100 Front Circle seats (priced £98 each, plus booking fee) for the Last Night of the Proms will be allocated by Open Ballot, which closes at midnight on Thursday 10 July. Please enter the ballot online or complete the official ballot form at bbc.co.uk/promstickets.

General availability for the Last Night

Any remaining tickets for the Last Night will go on sale at 9am on Friday 18 July by phone or online only. Only one application (for a maximum of two tickets) can be made per household. There is exceptionally high demand for Last Night tickets, but returns occasionally become available.

Promming (standing) at the Last Night

Season Promming Passes include admission to the Last Night. A limited allocation of Last Night standing tickets (priced £8, including booking fee) are also reserved for Prommers who have attended five or more concerts. They are eligible to purchase one ticket each for the Last Night on presentation of their used tickets (which will be retained) at the Box Office. For details, see bbc.co.uk/promstickets.

A limited number of Promming tickets are available on the Last Night itself (priced £8 including booking fee, one per person). No previous ticket purchases are necessary.

Royal Albert Hall

Kensington Gore, London SW7 2AP
www.royalalberthall.com • 020 7070 4441

The Royal Albert Hall of Arts and Sciences was officially opened by Queen Victoria on 29 March 1871. When, in 1867, Victoria laid the foundation stone for the building, she announced that it was to be named after her husband, Prince Albert, who had died six years earlier.

The Hall has hosted 25 suffragette meetings, and many of the world's leading figures in music, dance, sport and politics have appeared on its stage. These include Winston Churchill, Emmeline Pankhurst, the Dalai Lama and Nelson Mandela, as well as members of the royal family and world leaders.

The BBC Proms has called the Royal Albert Hall its home since 1941, after the Queen's Hall was gutted by fire in an air-raid. The Hall has since hosted over 4,500 Proms concerts.

Latecomers
Latecomers will only be admitted if and when there is a suitable break in the performance.

Security
Please do not bring large bags to the Royal Albert Hall. All bags and visitors will be subject to security checks as a condition of entry.

It is not permitted to bring food or drink into the Royal Albert Hall. However, there are bars, cafes and restaurants on-site. Find out more at royalalberthall.com/visit/food-and-drink.

Children under 5
Everyone is welcome at the CBeebies Proms (25 August) and the Relaxed Prom (10 August). Out of consideration for audience and artists, we recommend that children attending other Proms are aged 5 and over.

Dress code
Come as you are: there is no dress code at the Proms.

Proms merchandise and programmes
Merchandise is available at Doors 6 and 12 and on the Rausing Circle level at Doors 4 and 8. Programmes are on sale throughout the building. Merchandise can be pre-ordered online at shop.royalalberthall.com. You can pre-order programmes when booking your tickets (if booking after the onsale day) or via the link on your Print at Home tickets.

Access
See page 153 for access details.

South Kensington (Piccadilly, Circle & District Lines); Gloucester Road (Piccadilly, Circle & District Lines); High Street Kensington (Circle & District Lines)

Enjoy a wide range of food and drink from two hours before each concert – see royalalberthall.com

Cloakroom available. A charge per item applies. Cloakroom season tickets are also available *(conditions apply – see royalalberthall.com)*

The Fire Station, Sunderland
24 July

High Street West, Sunderland SR1 3HA
www.thefirestation.org.uk • 0191 570 0007

- 🚉 Sunderland
- 🍺 Bars on site; food and drink available
- 🧥 Cloakroom available tbc
- ♿ Wheelchair-accessible
- 🐕 Guide and assistance dogs welcome; please let venue know in advance
- **ALS** Assisted listening system

The Glasshouse International Centre for Music
25–27 July

St Mary's Square, Gateshead NE8 2JR
www.theglasshouseicm.org • 0191 443 4661

- 🚉 Newcastle Central (National Rail; Metro); Gateshead (Metro)
- 🍺 Bars on site; food and drink available
- 🧥 Cloakroom available
- ♿ Wheelchair-accessible
- 🐕 Guide and assistance dogs welcome

Ulster Hall, Belfast
8 August

34 Bedford Street, Belfast BT2 7FF
www.ulsterhall.co.uk • 028 9033 4455

- 🚉 Great Victoria Street (NI Railways)
- 🍺 Bars on site
- ♿ Wheelchair-accessible
- 🐕 Guide and assistance dogs welcome

Bristol Beacon
22–24 August

Trenchard Street, Bristol BS1 5AR
www.bristolbeacon.org • 0117 203 4040

- 🚉 Bristol Temple Meads (National Rail); city centre bus stops are 250m from the venue, where most bus services stop
- 🍺 Bars on site; food and drink available
- 🧥 Cloakroom available
- ♿ Wheelchair-accessible
- 🐕 Guide and assistance dogs welcome
- 🦻 Hearing loop system

Venues

**St George's
Bristol**
23 August

Great George Street, Bristol BS1 5RR
www.stgeorgesbristol.co.uk • 0117 929 4929

≋ Clifton Down; Bristol Temple Meads (National Rail)

🥤 Bars on site; food and drink available

♿ Wheelchair-accessible

🐕 Guide and assistance dogs welcome

🦻 Hearing loop system

**St George's Hall,
Bradford**
7 September

Bridge Street, Bradford BD1 1JT
www.bradford-theatres.co.uk/st-georges-hall • 01274 432000

≋ Bradford Interchange

🥤 Bar on site

♿ Wheelchair-accessible

🐕 Guide and assistance dogs welcome

Access at the Royal Albert Hall

All disabled concert-goers (and one companion) receive a 50% discount on all Proms tickets (excluding £8 Promming tickets). To book, call the Access Information Line *(see opposite)* or purchase in person at the Royal Albert Hall.

Wheelchair spaces and platform	All Proms
Guide and assistance dogs welcome	All Proms
AD Audio description **BSL** British Sign Language-interpreted Proms	26 July (The Traitors) 10 August (Relaxed Prom) 16 & 17 August (Shostakovich by Heart) 25 August (CBeebies Proms)
R Relaxed performances	10 August (Relaxed Prom) 25 August (CBeebies Proms)
ALS Assisted listening service	All Proms
LP Large-print programmes	All Proms; large-print programmes must be pre-ordered *(see page 155)*

ACCESS INFORMATION LINE

020 7070 4410 (9am–5pm, weekdays)

Full information on the facilities offered to disabled concert-goers at the Royal Albert Hall is available at royalalberthall.com or by calling the Access Information Line. The Hall has a Silver award from the Attitude is Everything Charter of Best Practice.

Throughout the Proms season at the Royal Albert Hall 12 spaces will be available to book for wheelchair-users and companions on a designated wheelchair platform situated in front of Loggia Boxes 31–33. Depending on the Prom, between 18 and 25 additional spaces for wheelchair-users and companions will be available in the Stalls and the Circle. To book, call the Access Information Line or visit the Royal Albert Hall Box Office in person.

For information on wheelchair spaces available for the Last Night of the Proms via the Five-Concert Ballot, see page 149.

The Gallery can accommodate up to four wheelchair-users. Some accessible seats in the Arena, Choir and Gallery (£8, including booking fee) are available to Prommers who are unable to stand. See bbc.co.uk/proms for details.

Ramped venue access is available at Doors 1, 3, 8, 9 and 12. The most convenient set-down point for vehicle arrival is near Door 3. Public lifts are located at Doors 1 and 8. All bars and restaurants are wheelchair-accessible.

Unisex wheelchair-accessible toilets are located as follows: *Level -1*: Door 1; *Ground Floor*: Door 4 porch, Door 8 porch and Door 12; *Level 1*: Door 4; *Level 2*: Door 4; *Level 3*: Door 8; *Level 5*: Door 1.

Transfer wheelchairs are available for customer use, subject to availability. The Hall has busy corridors and therefore visitors using mobility scooters are asked to enter via Door 3 or Door 8 and will be offered a transfer wheelchair on arrival.

Mobility scooters can be stored in designated places. The Hall is unable to offer charging facilities for scooters.

A limited number of car parking spaces close to the Hall can be reserved by disabled concert-goers; contact the Access Information Line to book.

Guide and assistance dogs are welcome. The Royal Albert Hall's stewards will be happy to look after your dog while you enjoy the concert. Please let us know in advance so we can arrange this for you.

To request any of the above services, call the Access Information Line or complete an accessibility request form online at royalalberthall.com 48 hours before you attend. Alternatively you can make a request upon arrival at the Information Desk at Door 6, subject to availability.

British Sign Language-interpreted Proms

BSL Seven Proms (both performances of The Traitors, the Relaxed Prom, both performances of Shostakovich's Fifth by Heart and both performances of the CBeebies Proms) will be BSL-interpreted. You can book tickets for these online in the usual way. If you require good visibility of the signer, choose the Stalls Signer Area when selecting tickets, or request by calling the Access Information Line.

Relaxed Proms

R BBC Proms relaxed performances (the Relaxed Prom and the CBeebies Proms) are designed to suit individuals or groups who feel more comfortable attending concerts in a relaxed environnment. These events offer a relaxed attitude to movement and noise and audience members are free to leave and re-enter the auditorium at any point. There will be chill-out areas, where spaces are made for anyone needing a bit of quiet time before or during the performance. For full details, visit bbc.co.uk/proms. Visual Information Guides for these concerts will be made available closer to the start of the season on the individual concert event pages. Visit bbc.co.uk/proms for details.

Assisted listening service and audio-described Proms

ALS
AD The Royal Albert Hall is equipped with a digital assisted listening system, delivering high-quality, reliable and interference-free audio to every seat in the auditorium. Six Proms (both performances of The Traitors, the Relaxed Prom, both performances of Shostakovich's Fifth by Heart and both performances of the CBeebies Proms) will be audio-described. Receiver packs and headphones for assisted listening services and audio-described performances are available from the Door 6 Information Desk. Customers are also welcome to use their own headphones (3.5mm minijack required).

See pages 151–152 for access information regarding Proms not at the Royal Albert Hall

> **❝** Having a dedicated wheelchair platform makes visiting the Proms so enjoyable and easy. From arrival at the Royal Albert Hall to getting to your 'seat', everything you need is nearby and really accessible, and the staff at the Hall are so helpful. I am very much looking forward to next season.

Antonia Stoneman, Proms audience member

Wheelchair platform at the Royal Albert Hall

For further information, please visit bbc.co.uk/proms. If you would like to discuss additional access requirements, call the Access Information Line (020 7070 4410; 9am–5pm, weekdays).

BBC Proms Festival Guide – Braille and large-print formats

Braille versions of this Festival Guide are available in two parts, 'Articles' and 'Concert Listings/Booking Information', priced £4.99 and £5 respectively. For more information and to order, call the RNIB Helpline on 0303 123 9999.

LP A text-only large-print version of this Festival Guide is available, priced £9.99. To order, call Deborah Fether on 07716 225658, or email PromsPublications@ bbc.co.uk. (Allow 10 working days for delivery.)

The Guide is also available to purchase as an eBook from Amazon and as both an eBook and ePDF from Bloomsbury. Both formats are compatible with screen readers and text-to-speech software. Visit amazon.co.uk or bloomsbury.com/uk for details.

Concert programmes in large print

LP Large-print concert programmes can be pre-ordered for collection on the night (at the same price as standard programmes), if ordered at least five working days in advance.

Large-print sung texts and librettos (where applicable) are available with the purchase of a standard programme, if ordered at least five working days in advance. This excludes surtitled Proms, for which librettos are not printed.

To order, call Deborah Fether on 07716 225658, or email PromsPublications@bbc.co.uk. Programmes and texts will be left for collection at the Door 6 Merchandise Desk one hour before the concert begins.

A Royal Albert Hall steward will be happy to read the concert programme to visually impaired visitors. Call the Access Information Line (020 7070 4410) or complete an accessibility request form online at royalalberthall.com 48 hours before you attend.

Access on BBC TV and iPlayer

A number of televised Proms, including the CBeebies Proms, will be broadcast with audio description and British Sign Language. Please see bbc.co.uk/proms for details.

Access

HERE AT AURIENS, YOU JUST KNOW...

...there will always be a friend here to hit the high notes with.

AURIENS

CHELSEA

Auriens Chelsea offers an exceptional lifestyle in 56 spacious, elegant apartments for the over 65s, overlooking Chelsea's King's Road. Enjoy a warm and welcoming community with a dedicated team who go the extra mile for your wellbeing and offer support tailored to your needs. Prices from £2.75m. Other fees apply.

To find out what makes Auriens as unique as the individuals who live here please get in touch.

020 4538 5658
auriens.com

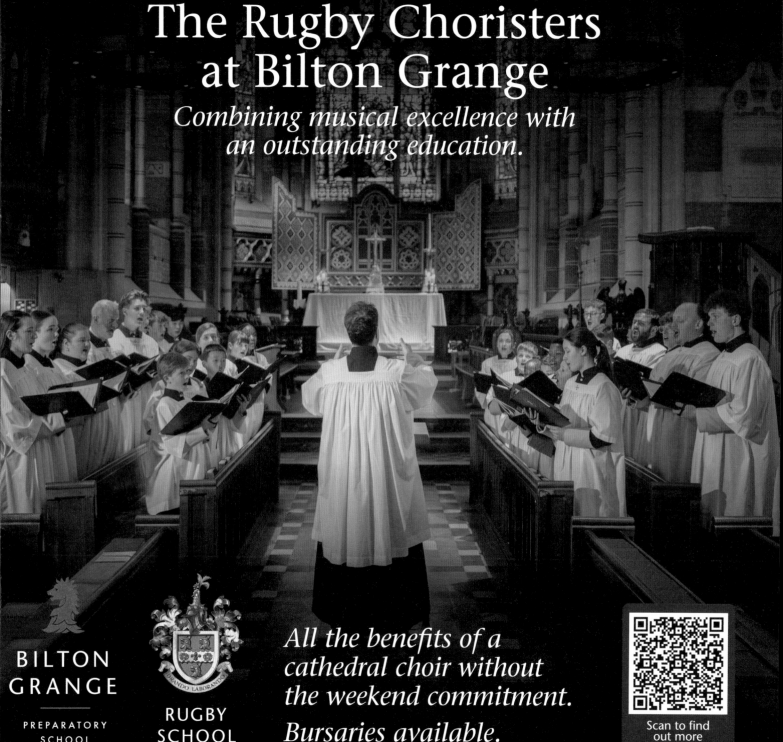

ROYAL ALBERT HALL

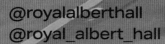

@royalberthall
@royal_albert_hall

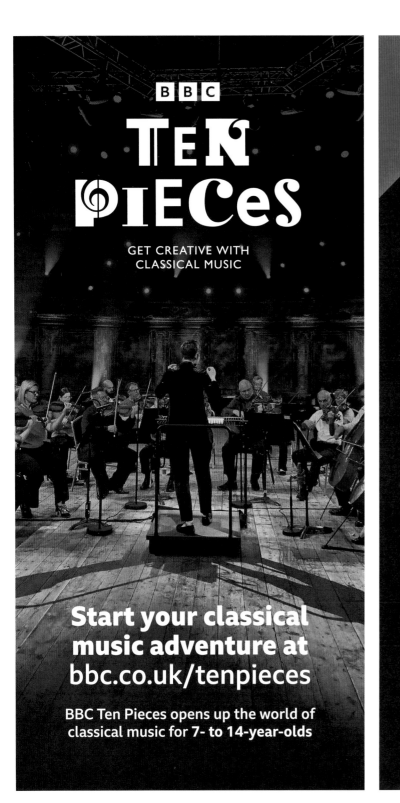

Index of Artists

Index of Artists

Index of Works

P@ refers to Proms Across the UK (see pages 142–146)

P@Belfast Friday 8 August
P@Bradford Sunday 7 September
P@Bristol Proms Bristol, Friday 22 – Sunday 24 August
P@Gateshead Proms Gateshead, Friday 25 – Sunday 27 July
P@Sunderland Thursday 24 July

* first performance at a BBC Henry Wood Promenade Concert

BBC Proms

Controller, BBC Radio 3 and BBC Proms Sam Jackson

Director of Artistic Planning, BBC Proms Hannah Donat

Head of Arts and Classical Music TV Suzy Klein

Commissioning Editor, TV Stephen James-Yeoman

Commissioning Editor, Live Music, BBC Radio 3 Emma Bloxham

Head of Marketing, Learning and Publications Kate Finch

Business Sanoma Evans (Business Advisor), Tricia Twigg, Rebecca Short (Business Co-ordinators)

Learning Melanie Fryer, Laura Mitchell (Producers), Siân Bateman, Catherine Humphrey (Assistant Producers)

Live Events and Planning Helen Heslop (Head of Live Events), Alys Jones (Creative Producer), Grace Fearon, Helen MacLeod, Jo de Sa, Shannon St Luce, Charlotte Sandford (Event Producers), Alexander Maxted, Lucy Rahim, Michael Triggs, Marianne Tweedie (Assistant Event Producers)

Marketing Emily Caket (Manager), Chloe Jaynes (Executive), Branwen Thistlewood (Co-ordinator)

Press and Communications George Chambers (Head of Communications, Classical Music), Jo Hawkins (Communications Manager), Freya Edgeworth (Publicist)

Commercial Rights & Business Affairs Emma Barrow, Alex Bradish, Sarah Bredl-Jones, Carol Davies, Frances Dougherty, Geraint Heap, Wendy Nielson, Ashley Smith, Daniel Williams

Television Production Livewire Pictures Ltd

BBC Proms Publications

Publishing Manager Christine Webb
Editorial Manager Edward Bhesania
Sub-Editor Timmy Fisher
Publications Designer Reenie Basova
Junior Publications Designer Jane Lochrie
Publications Co-ordinator Deborah Fether

Advertising Cabbells (020 3603 7930); cabbells.co.uk
Cover illustration Benedikt Luft/BBC Creative/BBC
Published by BBC Proms Publications, Room 3015, Broadcasting House, London W1A 1AA
Distributed by Bloomsbury Publishing, 50 Bedford Square, London WC1B 3DP

Printed by APS Group

APS Group holds ISO 14001 environmental management, FSC® and PEFC certifications. Printed using vegetable-based inks on FSC-certified paper. Formed in 1993 as a response to concerns over global deforestation, FSC (Forest Stewardship Council®) is an independent, non-governmental, not-for-profit organisation established to promote the responsible management of the world's forests. For more information, please visit www.fsc.org.

In line with the BBC's sustainability strategy, the BBC Proms is actively working with partners and suppliers towards being a more sustainable festival.

ISBN 978-1-912114-20-7   © BBC 2025. All details correct at time of going to press.

Proms 2025 Calendar

Mon		**21 Jul** — **Mahler's Seventh** 7.30pm • T. Coult, Mahler Clayton, BBC PO/Storgårds		**28 Jul** — **Beethoven and Birtwistle** 7.30pm • Birtwistle, Beethoven BBC SSO/R. Wigglesworth	
Tue		**22 Jul** — **Berlioz's 'Symphonie fantastique'** 7.30pm • R. Strauss, M. Simpson, Berlioz Shibe, BBC PO/Bihlmaier		**29 Jul** — **Arooj Aftab and Friends** 7.30pm Aftab, Maalouf, BBC SO/Buckley	
Wed		**23 Jul** — **French Night** 6.30pm • Ravel, *etc.* Goosby, Orchestre National de France/Măcelaru	**Boulez & Berio** ☾ 10.15pm • soloists, IRCAM, Ensemble intercontemporain/Bleuse	**30 Jul** — **Rachmaninov's Second Piano Concerto** 7.30pm • Bacewicz, Rachmaninov, Lutosławski Kholodenko, BBC NOW/Otaka	
Thu		**24 Jul** — **Mendelssohn's Violin Concerto** 7.30pm • Stravinsky, Mendelssohn, A. Davis, R. Strauss Hadelich, BBC SO/Oramo	**♀ Sunderland** 8pm • 'Round Midnight with Soweto Kinch	**31 Jul** — **Rachmaninov and Copland** 6.30pm • Barraine, Copland, A. Shaw, Rachmaninov Fröst, BBC PO/Weilerstein	**Arvo Pärt at 90** ☾ 10.15pm • A. Pärt, G. Grigorjeva, Rachmaninov, J. S. Bach, Tormis Estonian PCC/Kaljuste
Fri	**18 Jul** — **First Night of the Proms 2025** 7pm • Bliss, Mendelssohn, Sibelius, E. Wallen, Vaughan Williams Batiashvili, Singh, Finley, BBC Singers, BBC SC, Members of London Youth Choirs, BBC SO/Oramo	**25 Jul** — **Beethoven's Fifth** 6.30pm • Rameau, Saint-Saëns, J. Capperauld, Beethoven Kantorow, Scottish Chamber Orchestra/Emelyanychev	**♀ Gateshead** ☾ 9.15pm • Robert Ames and Royal Northern Sinfonia RNS/Ames	**1 Aug** — **Yunchan Lim Plays Rachmaninov** 7.30pm • J. Adams, Rachmaninov, Berio Lim, BBC Singers, CBSO/Yamada	
Sat	**19 Jul** — **The Great American Songbook and Beyond with Samara Joy** 7pm Samara Joy, Samara Joy Octet, BBC CO/Hazama	**26 Jul** — **The Traitors** AD BSL ☀ 3pm & 7.30pm Winkleman, BBC Singers, BBC SSO/Ní Bhroin **♀ Gateshead** ☀ 5.30pm **The Sorrow Songs** Angeline Morrison	**♀ Gateshead** 7.30pm • J. S. Bach, Mendelssohn soloists, CRNS, HCS, VOTRE, RNS/Sousa	**2 Aug** — **Viennese Whirl** ☀ 11am J. Strauss II, Josef Strauss, Korngold, Stolz, Dostal, Lehár, Kálmán Morley, BBC CO/ Helsing	**Mahler's 'Resurrection' Symphony** 8pm • Mahler Eriksmoen, D'Angelo, Hallé Choir, Hallé Youth Choir, Hallé/Wong
Sun	**20 Jul** — **Vivaldi and Bach** ☀ 11am Vivaldi, J. S. Bach, Avison, Marcello, Matteis Jr Le Consort/Langlois de Swarte	**Ravel's Piano Concerto for the Left Hand** 7.30pm Shostakovich/Atovmyan, Ravel, Walton McCarthy, Bournemouth SO/M. Wigglesworth	**27 Jul** — **Mozart and Bruckner** 7.30pm • R. Wigglesworth, Mozart, Bruckner Batsashvili, BBC SSO/R. Wigglesworth **♀ Gateshead** ☀ 1.30pm & 4pm CBeebies Prom: Wildlife Jamboree RNS	**♀ Gateshead** ☀ 3pm • T. Sorey, C. Miller, Boulez Shibe *et al*/Cemin	**3 Aug** — **Soul Revolution** 7.30pm Nelson, BBC CO/Bartholomew-Poyser	